# PAINTING MINIATURES FOR THE
## American Civil War

# PAINTING MINIATURES FOR THE
## American Civil War

STEVE BARBER

THE CROWOOD PRESS

First published in 2018 by
The Crowood Press Ltd
Ramsbury, Marlborough
Wiltshire SN8 2HR

www.crowood.com

British Library Cataloguing-in-Publication Data
A catalogue record for this book is available from the British Library.

ISBN 978 1 78500 509 1

**Acknowledgements**
All the miniatures featured in this book are by Steve Barber Models and are available from www.stevebarbermodels.com.

I could not have written this book without the invaluable help of the following people: Karen, Zachary, George and Valerie Angell, and Joel.

Frontispiece: A Union battery commander. The standard bearer was a simple conversion. Flag by GMB design. Painted by Steve Barber.

Typeset by Shane O'Dwyer, Swindon, Wiltshire

Printed and bound in India by Parkson's Graphics

# CONTENTS

The commander of a Union artillery battery surveys the scene before him.

*FLAGS ARE BY GMB DESIGNS. MINIATURES PAINTED BY STEVE BARBER.*

# Preface

I DISCOVERED PAINTING MODEL soldiers back in my early teens. I had no idea what I was doing at first, as I had hardly any painting references to use: all I knew was that I enjoyed painting and collecting them. Much of my pocket money went on my new hobby. There was a wargames shop in a nearby town, so I would save up and pester my parents to take me there. These trips continued over the next few years, and slowly but surely I started to amass a decent collection, of which I was duly proud. I remember reading a few painting articles in a wargames magazine, which inspired me to think about how I painted. Like most things, it is practice that really makes the difference, and the more I painted, the better I felt my painting became.

After I had finished school I started an apprenticeship in the printing industry. I have an uncle who worked for a top national newspaper, and to me, it seemed he had done well from that work, so I thought it was a good, steady job to get into. That didn't go as planned, though, as five years later I was made redundant, and over the following year I wasn't able to find another job in the printing industry. This was mainly due to the massive changes that were happening, such as the introduction of computer technology. It was a difficult time, and I was turned down for every job I went to, including cleaning floors (due to lack of experience!). Little did I realize at the time, but in fact this turned out to be an opportunity for me. Without that setback I would never have got on the path I did, and wouldn't be writing this book, for certain!

Friends and my parents told me how good my painting was, so I placed an advert in a wargames

A Union brigade commander halts his men to reconnoitre a deserted farm.

*FLAGS ARE BY GMB DESIGNS. MINIATURES PAINTED BY STEVE BARBER.*

magazine advertising my miniature painting service. This brought in a flurry of painting commissions. I painted miniatures for customers for a year, over that time in several scales and most periods of history. The miniatures I did were always painted to a collector's standard, with lots of detail. Some of the money I had earned, I invested into a vacuum chamber. This machine meant that I could now cast walls and buildings in resin. So I set about learning how to make wargames' accessories, and sold quite a few of these, unpainted and painted. This extra work meant that I started to phase out painting commissions, as I didn't have the time for both.

I began trading these accessories at a few wargames shows, and these shows led to others. I met people within the hobby who were happy to share their knowledge with me, and as my confidence grew I started sculpting miniatures. My first was a 25mm miniature of Al Capone's bookkeeper. I was so pleased with the result! Once I knew that I could sculpt to a standard I was happy with, I made a whole range of 25mm gangsters. I found someone who would mould and cast them for me, then I paid for an advert and hoped that people would like them. It worked! People responded, and purchased enough for me to make other miniatures. Eventually this became the business that I have now, with a web shop that sells miniatures around the globe.

I couldn't have achieved any of this without the help of my family and friends. Steve Barber Models has always been a family-run business, with my step-dad consistently by my side helping me to build up the business to where it is today. Since the beginning, he has done most of the casting, and is still heavily involved. My mum cleans up the figures that my dad casts, my fiancée does the bookkeeping and photography, and even my youngest son likes to try his hand at painting Daddy's soldiers. I couldn't do this without them, and am very lucky to have such a supportive group of people around me. Certainly my business would not be where it is today without their support, advice and understanding.

It has been a long road full of twists and turns, but this hobby gave me hope at a time when I really needed some. It gave me something to focus on, and since has become a big part of my life. So I would like to pass on some of the knowledge I have learnt over the years, and hopefully will inspire you to paint and collect your own miniatures.

Crowood approached me in 2017 to ask if I would be willing to write a book about painting miniatures. They are a very established publisher, well known for producing a large and excellent range of 'how-to' books on subjects such as model railways, amongst others. At first I was hesitant about the idea of writing a book. After all, my days are quite full just running my business, and everything that is involved in writing a book is not to be taken on lightly. But after I had time to think about it properly, I realized it was an opportunity to inform others of some of the things I have learnt over the years.

This book isn't aimed at experienced painters, but is intended to help those who are thinking about painting miniatures for the first time, as well as those

A Union infantryman wearing backpack at shoulder-arms.
*MINIATURE PAINTED BY STEVE BARBER.*

who want to improve their own painting style. I hope that it will help readers to start painting miniatures, and will encourage them to join the growing ranks of wargamers around the world. So with that in mind, there are simple step-by-step tutorials aimed at teaching the basic styles for painting American Civil War miniatures. Of course, these styles could equally be used on other types of figure as well.

Why choose the American Civil War, I hear you say? Well, there are a number of reasons both practical and historical that are of interest to us. The ACW, as it is often known, has a large following of gamers, re-enactors, modellers and historians. This band of dedicated enthusiasts makes it very easy to find out the information you are trying to source about an obscure commander or regiment. From a wargaming perspective, it also makes it easy to find an opponent near you to game with, whichever army you end up choosing. That is always a bonus, as you won't end up having to paint both armies to play a game – which can be the case when you choose a more obscure period of history to recreate.

These are all excellent reasons in themselves, but it also happens to be one of my favourite periods of history. My own collection of ACW miniatures grows steadily, with new miniatures being added when I can find some time out of my hectic schedule to paint.

The practical reasons for choosing this period are that there is a plentiful supply of miniatures in most scales, covering most of the regiments that fought for both the Union and the Confederacy. The miniatures are both attractive and characterful, but also not as difficult to paint as, say, a Jacobite Highlander in tartan plaid. So it is possible to paint large armies of miniatures reasonably quickly. It is essential to have regiments with twenty to thirty figures in order to make the battlefield look more realistic. It's important to remember that you are supposed to be representing thousands of actual troops for most ACW battles, so when you are playing grand scale wargaming, the units need to have a enough figures in them to look right.

There were some small skirmishes, and these can be fought with just a small number of miniatures

The 1st Texas infantry advance past a church.
*THE FLAG IS BY FLAGS OF WAR. MINIATURES PAINTED BY STEVE BARBER.*

a side if the individual nature of skirmish gaming appeals to you more than grand scale wargaming. Figures in skirmish games need to be individually based, as they represent individuals in combat. This style of gaming can appeal more to painters, as they can concentrate on lavishing time and details on their miniatures, as fewer are required to play skirmish games. These small combats can also be played using bigger figures such as 40mm scale. These figures have a lot of detail on them and tend to be painted individually, unlike the smaller scales.

Wargames rulebooks are available to refight everything from skirmishes, to brigade, divisional or bigger sized battles. In fact there are now a lot of different rulebooks to choose from. Some are simplistic and quicker to learn, and others will contain every conceivable detail, meaning that games can be slower. It's just a question of which style of game suits your time and budget best. It's certainly worth remembering that it's no use wanting to fight grand scale battles if you really don't have the time to paint the hundreds or thousands of miniatures needed to refight those battles. That will just leave you frustrated when the project grinds to a halt, as friends or club members are waiting for you to finish your troops so a game can begin. A bit of realism at this stage can only be a good thing.

Then there are the historical reasons. The American Civil War was fought over quite a long timespan, from 1861 to 1865, and this gives plenty of opportunities for the gamer to refight historic battles such as Antietam and Gettysburg. There is an abundance of uniform information, as well as photographs of the actual participants.

Also, the men who filled the ranks of most of the regiments that fought in the Civil War were recently arrived immigrants, so it's incorrect to think of it as just an American conflict. The men who enlisted

A battery of Union 20pdr Parrott rifled cannons load their guns ready for action.

*MINIATURES PAINTED BY STEVE BARBER.*

Duryee's 5th New York Zouaves advance at the double quick towards the front line.

*FLAGS BY GMB DESIGNS. MINIATURES PAINTED BY STEVE BARBER.*

came from most European countries, and in many cases spoke only their native language. Some were escaping civil wars and turmoil in their homelands, such as the recent revolutions in Hungary and Italy. Immigrants from Ireland made up the ranks of a notable number of regiments on both sides, and some of the most famous regiments of the Civil War were Irish regiments. Native Americans also fought, for both the Union and the Confederacy. After Lincoln's emancipation speech thousands of escaped slaves also enlisted. It was a multi-national conflict in many ways.

Consequently the miniatures that make up the regiments often have real character about them. At the start of the war the uniforms were sometimes flamboyant and impractical, such as glamorous Zouave regiments, inspired by the French empire. Quite often these regiments changed to a more ordinary uniform once these initial uniforms had worn out, though there were notable exceptions to this, such as the famous Duryee's Zouaves. This regiment looks grand in miniature, with their gaudy red trousers and white turbans. Then there is the famous Iron Brigade,

with their black hats, or Wheat's Tiger Zouaves with their pin-stripe, baggy Zouave trousers. Therefore besides all the regular units to paint for your army there are numerous characterful regiments such these to add interest to your collection.

Over the coming pages we will look at the different painting styles in detailed, but easy to understand, step-by-step tutorials. We will look at basing techniques, and how to show off your finished miniatures to their best, as well as how to paint buildings and convert your own miniatures. Where possible I have presented some of the finest products available to help you paint your ACW armies, from tools to flags and from paint to figures.

My intent is always to show you how to achieve good and realistic results when painting your armies, rather than how to paint single showcase miniatures. So whatever your motive for reading this book, whether it be collecting, gaming or just looking, I hope that you will find some useful ideas, techniques and inspiration within these pages to help you paint American Civil War miniatures and enjoy the hobby of wargaming!

# 1 Preparation

## SELECTING THE RIGHT MINIATURES

You may already know the scale you prefer, and may be set on that one, in which case it may be hard to change your mind. But when embarking on a new project it is always worth thinking about figure scale – and for those of you who are new to the hobby, choosing the right scale can seem daunting. The main thing is to look at the time, budget and space that you currently have. There is no point in choosing a scale that is unrealistic; most of us quickly become disheartened if it looks as if we might not finish what we have started. So have a good think about your project before you begin.

Think also about the space you have available to store and use your armies. If you don't have enough room for a games table at home there are plenty of wargames clubs around that would welcome new members, so there should be somewhere to show off and use your new army. The other benefit of going to a club is that you will find like-minded people there with whom you can discuss the hobby, and from whom you can learn. This can be invaluable to a beginner, and can help prevent you making the same mistakes as others have done.

The next decision you have to make is to decide the scale of your chosen army. The main scales of miniatures used for wargaming are 28mm, 20mm, 15mm, 10mm and 6mm. Larger figures than this, such as 40mm, are also available, but these tend to be used more for skirmish games and dioramas rather than big battle wargaming. At first glance to a beginner this can seem an overwhelming choice.

A Confederate regiment advances into action. *FLAGS ARE BY GMB DESIGNS. MINIATURES PAINTED BY STEVE BARBER.*

Before beginning on a project it is well worth thinking carefully about the right scale for you, rather than changing your mind later on after you have already invested time and money in your project. Although there are many scales, there are four that are more commonly used for wargaming, so we will examine the advantages of each.

## 28mm Scale

These days, 28mm is probably the scale that has the highest number of collectors and gamers. This is partly because of the abundance of high quality miniatures that are available now. At this size, fingers and facial details are easily distinguishable from a reasonable distance, yet the figures are still small enough to have fairly large battles on a reasonable sized table. 28mm is also well supported in terms of buildings and terrain features, that will help bring your battlefield to life. I prefer to paint and collect 28mm because of the enjoyment of painting the details on each miniature. This is a painter's scale. And as a result miniatures can be painted in several different styles at this size. This is ideal, as there is bound to be a style that suits you. The downside of 28mm is the space they take up, and as they are more substantial they cost a bit more.

## 15mm Scale

15mm scale is also well supported, so there are plenty of figures, printed flags, scenery and other items for the wargamer. The 15mm scale used to be the most popular scale amongst wargamers, but has become less popular than the 28mm scale; however, it still does have a large following. It is a lovely scale and perfectly suited to big battle wargaming. Large battles can be fought using 15mm miniatures and they paint up fast. The level of detail on figures is high and they can make great looking armies. 15mm miniatures can be painted with a simplified version of the layering technique but most people would paint in a similar style to 10mm and 6mm figures. Therefore they are quick to paint but are detailed and nice to look at.

## 10mm Scale

10mm is a relatively new scale to the hobby. It's possible to get a higher level of detail on a miniature of this size than a 6mm miniature, yet they are still small enough for very large battles. 10mm figures do look excellent en masse and tend mostly to be painted in the same way as you would paint a 6mm miniature. There is no real need to do layer painting at this scale, as this technique is more to create light and shade, which is possible to do on a small figure, but no one will see it even if you could do it. Simple wash techniques, or allowing the black undercoat to create lines around areas by not painting to the edge of an area, are the best ways to create depth. There are some lovely figures available for gamers who prefer smaller scale miniatures.

## 6mm Scale

Like their 10mm counterparts, 6mm miniatures are ideal for regiments comprising larger numbers of figures. This scale of miniature is for grand scale wargaming, big battles formed of large regiments. The figures do have a surprising level of detail on them, but at arm's length when played with during a game the detail of individual miniatures is not what this scale is about. Regiments can be made much larger and more realistic looking. Games are usually played at corps or army level rather than with brigades or divisions. One of the advantages of 6mm and 10mm scale is that they don't take up a lot of space to store, and they cost less than the larger scales, although you do need more of them.

## Choosing Figures

Once you have decided on the scale, it's just a case of finding the style of figure you like. Personally I like collecting 28mm-scale figures; the miniatures used throughout this book are 28mm scale and are produced by Steve Barber Models. They are cast in white metal and are very easy to assemble. It does help if a figure has a certain amount of raised detail on it, as this definition makes it much easier and more enjoyable to paint. So, when sculpting a range of ACW miniatures I wanted to incorporate this feature into my miniatures.

I also wanted them to have individual characters, so these miniatures have been designed with separate heads. This, along with a system of separate legs and torsos that plug together, means the figures you create for your armies can be unique. They are

The 63rd New York infantry prepares for battle. This regiment was part of the famous Irish brigade that fought for the Union. *FLAGS ARE BY GMB DESIGNS. MINIATURES PAINTED BY STEVE BARBER.*

designed to allow one pack to be mixed with another pack, meaning the possibilities for conversion are simply down to your imagination and some historical research. The range is now huge, and includes artillery and generals.

## BOOKS AND UNIFORM GUIDES

Before you can start painting you will need to know what colours to paint your miniatures. Although we are perhaps fortunate enough to be able to Google anything these days and track down information on uniforms, it is still useful to have a good book or two on the subject. Don Troiani's books on uniforms of the Civil War are excellent; the colour plates are gorgeous and inspiring to paint from. Keith Rocco is another excellent artist, so look out for books containing his work. Osprey Publishing produce a considerable number of books on the American Civil War and many other periods of history, which are ideal for wargamers and history enthusiasts alike. These books are small but concise and contain a

number of colour plates in the centre of the book. They make great historical reference books as well as uniform guides. As miniature painters we are very fortunate that this part of history is well covered by so many talented artists and writers. Without them our hobby would be much harder!

## FINDING SUITABLE TOOLS, BRUSHES AND PAINTS

### Quality Paints

Over the years I have tried many types of paints, varnish and brushes with mixed results. Today there are some great ranges of hobby paints designed for the gamer. Alternatively, you can mix your own colours using artist's tube acrylic paints. These are water based and it is very easy to mix your own paints. Doing this can give excellent results as it is possible to mix all the colours you need in as many shades as you desire. Small plastic pots are ideal to store the paint in, and it will last for a long time properly sealed. Each time it thickens up you can just

The Vallejo equestrian set has a great variety of colours that are perfect for painting horses.

FAR LEFT: The Vallejo Model Color range of paints is ideal for painting miniatures.

LEFT: A pot of Vallejo wash.

add a little water to the pot and shake it, and it will keep it going longer.

Vallejo is one of the best brands of paint designed specifically for the gamer. They produce a great range of high quality, water-based acrylic paints that are designed for wargaming and many other modelling hobbies. They have been making paints since 1965, when they first started making colours for cartoons. Their range is massive and covers just about every conceivable colour, so it is possible to buy ready-mixed colours for whatever army you have chosen to paint. The paints are sold in plastic bottles and are very easy to use; they cover well and are not grainy.

Vallejo also make washes and pigments, and have such an extensive range there is bound to be something that suits everyone.

I use a variety of paints depending on the effect I am trying to achieve. A large number of my paints are by Vallejo, but there are other leading makes in my collection as well. I also mix my own paints in old film plastic pots; these are opaque so they protect the paint from light. The pots are also well sealed, which prevents the paint from drying up.

To suit your own taste it will probably sometimes be necessary to mix your own colours. After all, the perception of colour is a very personal thing, and is rarely something people agree on. For example, Union Civil War jackets were in reality a very, very dark blue. I have often seen them painted in a rich French blue instead of the deep indigo the colour should be. This darkness in the blue jacket seems to offsets the sky blue trousers much better.

Some people use oil paints on their miniatures to good effect; oil washes in particular work very well. A very small amount of oil paint mixed with a lot of thinners will create your own oil wash, which can be used on certain areas to create a desired result. This can even work well over a whole figure, bringing out detail whilst adding a weathering effect at the same time.

Civil War miniatures work well with a somewhat weathered look to reflect the hardships often endured by the troops in the field. Modern day re-enactors are often a good source of information regarding what the troops of this conflict would really have looked like after months of hard campaigning in all weathers with limited supplies. Traditionally, wargaming figures tended to be painted to look smart, often in full dress uniforms without a speck of dirt in sight, but most collectors today favour a more realistic look. The appearance of troops who had been campaigning for months or years would, in many cases, be a long way from the smart uniforms in which they may have paraded at the start of the conflict.

Shoes in particular would wear out very quickly, and resupply could be a real problem. During the Napoleonic wars, Wellington's army fighting against Napoleon in Spain frequently did not have enough shoes, and many of the men often fought barefoot, looting from a fallen foe or even the local populace! The same supply problems were true of the American Civil War, especially for some of the southern states thought to have fought for the Confederacy.

## Selecting the Right Brushes

Besides choosing good paints and deciding how you want your troops to look, it is vital to find good brushes in order to paint your miniatures well. The brush needs to have a good pointed tip. Often in big stores the brushes are damaged where the plastic cover has been roughly put back. If the hairs are splayed out at the sides the brush will not come back to a good point and is useless for detail work.

The paintbrushes used exclusively throughout this book are by Vallejo. Their 'starter' set and their 'brushes for miniatures' set cover everything you will need for the techniques covered in this book. There is a dedicated dry-brushing brush as well as a size 2 for large areas of painting, and a selection of smaller sizes for different types of detail work.

### Caring for your Brushes
When you own good quality brushes it is important to know how to care for them. If you look after them

The 'starter' set of paint brushes by Vallejo.

The 'brushes for miniatures' set by Vallejo.

well they will last for quite a while, they will paint numerous miniatures, and will save you money. When painting, always wash the paint off the brush thoroughly in your water pot to avoid it drying hard on the hairs; once paint is clogged and hard it can be almost impossible to remove. Keeping the paint wet can help to avoid this beginning to happen: just give the brush a quick wash in the water every now and then, or dab a bit of water on the mixing palette.

The paintbrush sizes you will need are size 0 and size 1, and a couple of larger ones, one for applying varnish – and it is best to keep the brush just for this purpose – and the other for applying paint to large areas. This will be needed for horses and artillery. If you are using the dry-brushing technique, which is explained later in the section Painting Artillery, then you will need a larger brush just for dry brushing miniatures. The dry-brushing technique will do your brush no good at all, so if possible it is best always to use an old brush for this purpose.

## CLEANING UP MINIATURES FOR PAINTING
### Removing Flash and Mould Lines

To remove flash and mould lines you will need a scalpel or model knife – I use a scalpel with a 10a scalpel blade. This has a good long point, which is useful for getting into awkward places on a model. Alternatively you could use a model knife, which you can buy from a hobby shop, or online. You will also need a decent large file: this is the best way of removing the rough line sometimes to be found on the bottom of a figure, indicating where it was attached to the central reservoir during casting. Simply file this flat until the miniature can stand evenly on the base by itself.

To remove the mould lines on a miniature it's a question of almost brushing the sharp edge of the scalpel across the mould line. This may need to be repeated a few times until the area becomes slightly shiny. When doing this try not to remove any detail. If the mould line is over a detailed area it can be difficult to remove, and a certain amount of experience is required to know when you have achieved as much as you can. It's important not to press too hard during this process, to avoid breaking the blade. Great care must always be taken when using a scalpel as the blade is incredibly sharp, so only do so if you are able to control it safely. Used sensibly, a scalpel is an important tool for modellers.

Hopefully most miniatures produced these days shouldn't have too much flash on them, but if the mould has become too hot during casting then a small amount may occur. Thin flash is like a piece of

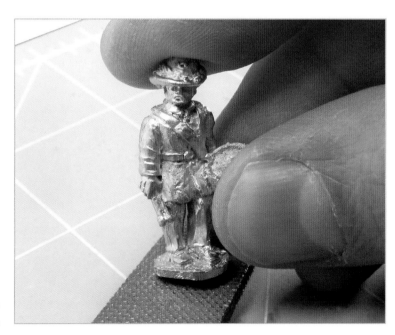

It is best to use a large file to file the base of the figure flat.

LEFT: Use a scalpel or model knife to scrape away the mould lines on a miniature.

BELOW: Loctite Precision glue.

tinfoil, and you should be able to remove it easily with a scalpel or model knife. If the flash is too thick it can be difficult to remove with a model knife, and repeated attempts might be required to remove it, a stage at a time. Ultimately if the flash is too thick then you might have to contact the manufacturer you purchased the figure from, as miniatures shouldn't need that much cleaning up.

## Gluing Miniatures Together

Depending on the material your chosen miniatures are made from, it is vital to use the right glue when gluing them together. Metal miniatures should glue together perfectly with superglue; I use Loctite Precision Superglue, which has a fine nozzle that is perfect for getting the glue into hard-to-reach areas. Because the nozzle is small it also means you don't end up getting more glue than you intend on to the model you are working on – spilled glue like this can clog up the details you are hoping to paint. Loctite Precision is perfect for avoiding this.

If you are gluing plastic miniatures together then it is vital to use plastic glue, otherwise the figures will not bond together correctly. Plastic glue essentially melts the two pieces of the model together so it should not come apart. It is therefore vital to position the pieces correctly, as once glued you

can't easily alter them. Also it is best not to use too much glue, as the melted plastic gloop will ooze out between the parts and can be smudged, and this is hard to remove.

## Filling Joins

The joins in some miniatures may need filling with putty before painting can begin. This is a simple process and nothing to be afraid of. I use 'green stuff' putty by Sylmasta for this process. Slice off a strip of equal amounts and roll the putty together until it makes an even green colour. A model tool with a tapered spoon-style head is the best to use to apply the putty. Model or clay sculpting tools should be available from most good art shops, or online.

Simply press the putty into the join and flatten it out using the sculpting tool. Smooth it over by putting some water on the tool, then smooth the tool across the putty. When you are happy that all the joins are filled without covering any of the figure's details, then leave the miniature to dry. It should take a couple of hours to harden properly. Then painting the miniature can begin!

# SETTING UP YOUR PAINT STATION

The advice given in the following paragraphs is learnt from years of experience of painting and sculpting. Much is common sense, but it's surprising how easy it is not to think about the way you are sitting because you are focused on the miniature you are working on, only to find you have, say, a painful back afterwards because you weren't seated properly.

You are more likely to paint regularly if you can leave all your paints set up in the same place; a desk or something similar is ideal if possible. If you have to set up everything each day the time this takes will eat into your painting session and may become a reason for you not to paint that day. Your painting area should be relaxing, and a pleasure to be in.

A good comfortable chair is essential. I prefer an upright padded chair, which I pull right under the table when painting. This helps to prevent my back from slouching, and gives my arms some support when painting. These few simple steps really help to prevent joint and muscle pain after longer spells of painting.

A small jar or pot of water to wash your paintbrushes in is essential, and another pot to store your brushes in is also a good idea. It is best to keep the plastic covers on your brushes when they are not in use, removing and replacing the covers carefully each time you use them. Replacing these carefully is essential to good brush care, to prevent hairs getting bent round in the cover; once this has happened it is almost impossible to get them straight again, and you will never regain the brush's point.

A ceramic tile as you might have in a bathroom or kitchen is perfect for mixing paint on, because the paint dries much more slowly on the shiny, non-porous surface. This is a good way to keep the colours you have mixed going for longer; just add a little water off your brush when the paint starts to thicken.

It is important to have a good craft table light to illuminate the work area, and the whiter the light, the better the result; it is essential to be able to discern the difference between darker shades. A Union soldier's jacket is very dark, and without good lighting in your work area it is much harder to tell the difference between the shades in such a colour. A white light also gives you a more accurate perception of the colour you are painting. So don't risk your eyes with poor lighting.

The Shesto LC8093 magnifying lamp has an excellent magnifying glass with a smaller, more powerful magnifier built into it. This extra magnification is perfect for those really fine details. It also has a very bright white light, ensuring that you see accurately the colours on the miniature you are painting. Decent lighting that is positioned above the object you are painting also helps prevent headaches from eye strain. If the light is at the side of the object rather than above it, this can strain your eyes, which will lead to headaches.

When painting regularly it is important to keep your work area tidy, as specks of dirt may end up getting in the paint or on your mixing tile or brush. Such 'housekeeping' may help avoid the situation where you discover an annoying lump underneath the paint and then have to remove it with a scalpel. I try to keep one area of my table just for drying, so all the figures I am working on stay in that one place at the back of my table.

I use plastic pots to paint figures on. Years ago, a photography shop that developed customers' holiday snaps was happy to give me a bag full of old camera film canisters, as they were normally thrown away; they are now available to buy online. I glue the miniatures to them each time using a small amount of superglue. Always take care when using this type of glue, as it is very strong.

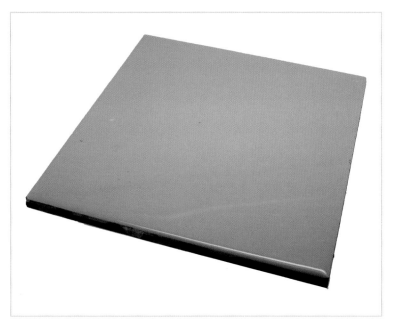

LEFT: A ceramic tile is ideal to mix your paints on.

BELOW: A plastic pot is perfect to fix miniatures to while painting.

It should be possible to reuse the pots many times. If you can't locate similar canisters, then any type of pot or wine cork would do just as well.

Another idea is to glue each miniature to the end of a wooden dowel; these are then placed in a glass jar to keep the figures upright. Smaller miniatures can be glued on to an ice-lolly stick or similar and then painted. Using this method it should be possible to glue at least eight figures in a row and still have enough room to grasp the stick with your fingers.

The main reason for gluing the miniature to something that you then hold is so that you don't chip or smudge any of the paint you have just applied. Also, if you are painting a lot of figures you can hurt your hands by gripping them tightly: tendonitis and RSI are just a couple of potential injuries caused by gripping the miniature itself or holding its base. Using a film pot puts less grip pressure on the tendons, and since using pots I haven't had the problems I used to get.

Once your painting station is all set up and you have decided how you will hold your miniatures whilst painting, then all you need to decide is which painting method you will use. The next chapters detail the different painting techniques that you can use to paint your American Civil War miniatures. There are two main styles for painting wargames

figures: layer painting and wash painting. A mixture of both techniques can also be used to good effect. This gives the benefits of the speed of wash painting, but the detail and depth of layer painting. Over the next three chapters I will cover those styles in detail.

## INTRODUCTION TO LAYER PAINTING

Layer painting is the process of painting a miniature by building up successive paler layers of paint. This style of painting figures has been around for quite a few years and is widely used amongst wargamers today. The idea of this painting technique is that the layers gradually get lighter in shade and finer in application. These layers create light and shade on the model, and give extra depth to the colours you have used. It is up to you how many layers of paint you decide to use, but for wargaming purposes three or four is usually enough to give a great effect without it taking weeks to paint a single miniature.

Most wargamers want to paint armies, and not single figures for display, so there has to be some compromise on the standard of painting in view of the number of miniatures required for an army. As a result of this compromise, having three or four layers of shading is sufficient for most people. The techniques shown in this book are mainly aimed at helping novices learn how to begin painting wargames' miniatures for the purpose of creating

The 5th NYSM – or Duryee's Zouaves as they were also known – charge fearlessly towards the foe!
*FLAGS ARE BY GMB DESIGNS.*
*MINIATURES PAINTED BY STEVE BARBER.*

An example of layer painting.

is evenly covered. The miniature should then have the base coats applied to its main areas, such as jacket and trousers. These base coats are the darkest shade of each colour used. After this, the mid-tone and highlight layers are painted over raised areas of the model. These shades are each lighter than the last. How much lighter these shades should be is something of a personal choice.

Painting using this technique allows the recesses and natural folds on the miniature to act as shading, with the darker base coat still visible in the folds of the miniature. This use of the raised areas helps create natural light, so adding to the tonal range of each colour. The final highlight layer is usually a fine line in the centre of each raised area, giving brightness to each colour on the figure.

## Advanced Layer Painting

In the case of a collector's display piece, the miniature may have ten to twelve layers painted on each colour. On this type of figure the last layer is very pale, or almost white. This gives a considerable depth to the colours used, and when done well it gives a smooth transition through the shades of each colour. It can really make each colour pop out at you.

The important part of this technique, though, whether standard or advanced, is to allow the layer beneath the one you are currently painting to be visible. The only way to achieve this is to make each layer narrower and smaller, thereby allowing the previous shade still to be seen. Of course, this gets harder with each layer used, and does require considerable patience and a steady hand if a lot of layers are used on each colour. With numerous layers the difference between each shade of the colour becomes harder to differentiate, especially with dark colours. It ceases to become just base tone, mid-tone and highlights, as larger amounts of white or similar colours are added each time to create lighter and lighter shades.

So attempting advanced layer painting may not be for everyone, and probably not most wargamers, but if it is a question of individual fine quality miniatures for a collection, then this is undoubtedly the best method of painting to use. The advanced layer painting technique is often combined with the use of ink washes to help blend colours. On large areas of colour, retarders can be added to the paint

armies. Advanced versions of the main three painting techniques are mentioned throughout this book, but these pages are aimed more at showing the basic techniques required.

Painting an army requires painting figures in batches – ten is a good number. It is a fruitless task to paint one miniature at a time, and you can lose continuity of style doing this. Painting figures in batches means that all the repeating parts can be painted at the same time. So, for example, the trousers can be painted on all ten figures, and then the jackets, and so on. This saves a lot of time opening paints and washing brushes, and means that the colours remain consistent on the group you are painting. This is especially useful if you are using colours you are mixing yourself.

When using the layer painting process, the miniature is undercoated first. It is important that no metal is visible at this stage, and that the figure to blend the paint on the miniature rather than mix numerous shades on a palette and then add them to the model. Blending colours in this way requires practice and a wet palette, as once the pale colour is added, it's added, and there is no changing your mind and going back.

## The Paints Used in this Chapter

The paints used in this section are by Vallejo, from their extensive, fabulous range of model colours. These paints are acrylic, and so are water based and non-toxic, meaning you can clean your brushes with tap water. The fact that they are water based also means the residue cleans off the mixing tile easily, even if it has dried.

The paints are sold in plastic dropper bottles and so have to be poured on to the mixing tile before they can be used. The paints mix well by pouring some of each colour on to the tile and then combining them with a mixing brush. If the paint starts to thicken, then a few drops of water will make it fluid again. They dry fairly quickly once painted on the miniature. This allows the next colour to be put on straight after when using the layer painting technique.

If you need to slow the drying time for blending colours, then the paint can be mixed with a retarder, which Vallejo also produce.

I have chosen to use their American Civil War set, as it is an ideal place for the novice painter to start. The set has a great choice of colours for both the Union and the Confederacy, so you can just open it

The Vallejo American Civil War set is a good place to start when painting ACW miniatures.

The Vallejo flesh tones' set has a great range of colours in it.

up and start painting. I will also be using the flesh tones set that they make. This set has a great range of shades for Caucasian flesh and lips. I have also used a few colours from their Equestrian set, as the browns and natural colours in this set are excellent for all sorts of things besides horses. This is a set of paints that you will need anyway when it comes to painting cavalry.

The other individual colours I have used are Bone White, Stormy Blue and Gory Red from Vallejo's game colour range. These last two colours will become the base coats and shading for the main colours on this miniature. The Stormy Blue colour I find excellent for the base shade of the dark blue Union jackets. The Gory Red is a fabulous base shade for Zouave trousers.

STEP 1: Undercoating with black spray paint.

## PAINTING A UNION ZOUAVE MINIATURE IN TWELVE STEPS

This miniature is from Collis's Zouaves, the 114th Pennsylvania Volunteers, a regiment that fought with distinction for the Union during the Civil War. Its colonel also received the Medal of Honor for his actions. The regiment was decimated during the Battle of Gettysburg, but continued to fight throughout the remainder of the Civil War. Its extravagantly colourful uniform makes it an easy choice for demonstrating the layer painting technique. The miniature was cleaned of any mould lines, assembled and glued together, and then glued on to a film canister using Loctite superglue.

### Step 1: Undercoating
*Colours:* Black spray paint

The first stage of the process is to undercoat the miniature. This first step is important, as it will help the later layers of paint to adhere to the metal model. The chosen colour of undercoat also helps to influence the overall finished effect of the figure: it is essentially your canvas. I prefer a black undercoat, because any small area you miss later will just look like a dark shadow. Car spray paint in a matt black is good for this as it covers well in a smooth layer and is cost effective.

Spraying is a fast way of undercoating a large number of figures at once – though always use spray paint outside due to the fumes. When spraying, group the miniatures close together on newspaper as this will minimize waste paint. Spray one side at a time, leaving a good ten minutes before turning them over to paint the other side. It may take a couple of coats on each side to give a good even coat. Try not to use too much paint at once as painting in thin layers gives the best result.

### Step 2: Clothing base shades
*Colours:* Stormy Blue, Gory Red,
Deep Sky Blue and Extra Dark Green

The first job to do after the undercoat has dried is to apply the base shades to trousers, jacket and fez. Paint the Zouave jacket and shirt in Stormy Blue mixed with a small amount of black: this is to darken down the base shade even further. Then paint the

trousers and fez in Gory Red, and next the cuffs and sash, using a mix of Stormy Blue and small amount of Extra Dark Green and Sky Blue. This produces a good murky green/blue colour for the base shade for these areas. Apply the paint as accurately as you can, though it doesn't matter if there are a few mistakes at this stage as they can always be tidied up later.

### Step 3: Musket and water-bottle base shades
*Colours:* Flat Brown, Beige Brown
and Leather Brown

At this stage you can begin applying the base shade to equipment, such as musket woodwork and leather belts. In the case of this miniature, many of the belts are black and are already painted when the miniature was undercoated black. This saves time, and it is worth trying to keep the straps neat and free of other colours as the belts will then only need the highlight stage to be finished. For the woodwork on the musket use Flat Brown for its base shade.

STEP 2: Clothing base shades.

STEP 3: Musket and water-bottle base shades.

STEP 4: Clothing mid-tones and
water-bottle highlight are added.

STEP 5: Clothing highlights
and detailing.

After this the last piece of equipment to paint is the water bottle. Paint the base coat of the water-bottle cover using Beige Brown, also the two tiny areas of the cover just visible under the water-bottle strap. This is quite intricate, but it is attending to small details such as this that really helps complete the finished miniature. The final part of this stage is to paint the first shade on the water-bottle strap using Leather Brown.

### Step 4: Clothing mid-tones and water-bottle highlight
*Colours:* Carmine Red, Stormy Blue, Fire Orange, Blue, Deep Sky Blue, Extra Dark Green and Tan Earth
Next begin painting the second layers on all the clothing. For the trousers and fez use Carmine Red with a tiny amount of Fire Orange added to it. Paint the jacket and vest with Stormy Blue over the peaks of the creases in the material. At this stage also add the next shade to the cuffs and the sash, which

is a mix of Blue and Extra Dark Green and a small amount of Deep Sky Blue. Add the green colour because the blue sash this regiment used had a greenish tinge to it.

Then add the second layers to some of the equipment. Finish painting the water bottle: use Tan Earth for the highlight coat on the water-bottle cover, and paint the highlight coat in stripes to create texture on the flat surface; this allows some of the previous colour to show through. The Tan Earth colour provides a nice contrast to the previous shade.

### Step 5: Clothing highlights and detailing
*Colours:* Carmine Red, Fire Orange, Deep Sky Blue, Extra Dark Green, Dark Grey and Leather Brown
At this stage paint the third highlight on all the clothing areas. Mix equal amounts of Carmine Red and Fire Orange together to create the third and final shade for the trousers and fez. For the final shade for the cuffs and the sash mix Deep Sky Blue with a tiny

dash of Extra Dark Green to create the final highlight for the cuffs and sash. Then paint the first shade on the musket strap using Leather Brown. After that paint the highlights on the belt, haversack, cartridge box, cap box and shoes using Dark Grey. The final detail to add at this stage is to paint the piping on the Zouave jacket in Carmine Red. This is quite fine, and requires a steady hand and a very good detail brush.

### Step 6: Musket woodwork highlight and other details
*Colours:* Beige Brown, Sunny Skin Tone, Fire Orange, Tan Earth and Leather Brown

Next paint the wood effect on the musket. This is achieved by painting fine lines in a paler colour: in this case use Beige Brown. These contrasting lines give the appearance of grain in the wood. The lines need to be quite fine and a small distance apart, but they don't have to be too neat as wood can have an imperfect grain, which only adds to the realism. Then paint the highlight on the musket strap and on the

water-bottle strap using a mix of equal amounts of Leather Brown and Tan Earth.

At this stage you can begin to add some details to the miniature. Paint the first shade of the yellow band around the fez and the tassle in a mix of Sunny Skin Tone and a large amount of Fire Orange. The Sunny Skin Tone lightens and slightly dulls the orange and makes a good deep base colour for yellow. Add details to clothing once the main colour of the garment has all three shades completed. Also add the base colours to the gaiters around the figure's ankles. Paint the base shade of the brown lower part of the gaiter in Leather Brown. After this paint the base shade of the white top part of the gaiter in a mix of Bone White and Tan Earth.

### Step 7: Metallic base shades
*Colours:* Oily Steel and Blackfriars Deep Gold metallic paint

Paint all the metallic colours together, as you are then less likely to forget any small detail, which avoids

STEP 6: Musket woodwork and other details.

STEP 7: Metallic base shades.

having to go back and do them separately. Use Deep Gold to paint the base shade on all the gold details, including the belt buckles, the bayonet scabbard point and the badge on the cartridge box. Don't paint any base shade on the buttons because the highlight shade is sufficient on these small details.

Next paint the metalwork on the musket and bayonet in Oily Steel, also the plate on the butt of the musket, as well as the musket lock, trigger and the loops that hold the barrel on. This colour is an excellent base shade for the steel on the musket. Parts that need painting that are easily over looked are the water-bottle cap and the metal rings the strap goes through, and the clips that hold on the musket strap. Paint all these with Oily Steel.

## Step 8: Metallic highlights

*Colours:* Liquid Silver, Liquid Gold

Next paint the second highlight on all the silver and gold areas, once again keeping the area painted smaller than the previous layers so that some of the Oily Steel and Deep Gold can still be seen. I prefer to use Vallejo Liquid Gold and Silver for the final highlights on metallic areas as these paints really do give a great shine and realistic metallic finish. You will need an alcohol brush cleaner to clean your brushes when using these liquid colours, as these paints are not produced in the same way as the rest of their range. It's a good idea to keep one particular brush to use with metallic colours to avoid contaminating the next colour you use with any tiny particles that may still remain on the brush, even after cleaning.

## Step 9: Skin base shade and fez details

*Colours:* Dark Flesh, Flat Yellow, Beige Brown, White and Bone White

The next step is to paint the base shade of the skin tones. On this miniature apply Dark Flesh paint to the face, ears, the back of the neck and the hands. Apply the paint evenly, making sure black is not visible anywhere on the face and hands or between the fingers. It doesn't matter if a little gets on the hair, but be careful around areas you have already painted such as the collar, cuffs and fez.

STEP 8: Metallic highlights.

STEP 9: Skin base shade and fez details are added.

At this stage add a second colour to the yellow band on the fez and the tassel, using Flat Yellow; apply it to give a kind of dotted line effect around the band of the fez. This helps to give the appearance of small movements in the material as it catches the light. Paint the raised areas on the tassel and the cord that attaches it to the fez with the same colour.

Then paint a second colour to both parts of the gaiters. For the brown part use Beige Brown, and for the white part Bone White with a small amount of white added to it. White on its own is too bright and perfect looking to be used as it is, and things look more realistic if it is darkened slightly with another similar colour.

### Step 10: Skin mid-tones and other details
*Colours:* Basic Skin Tone, Flat Brown, Flat Yellow and White

Now paint the second layer of skin tones. Use a fine brush to pick out the cheeks, chin and eyebrows on the miniature's face using Basic Skin Tone. Continue this process on the fingers, knuckles and hands, making sure that all the raised areas of detail are painted in the second shade, and that the base colour is still visible in the creases and lines on the face and hands. Tidy up any mistakes with the Dark Flesh colour. Also at this point add a fine brown line on each eye slit: the paint should sit in the recess of the sculpture's eyes.

Finally apply the third highlight colour to the ends of the fez tassel, cord and around the fez band, using a mix of Flat Yellow with some white added to it.

### Step 11: Tidying up and piping highlights
*Colours:* Black, Carmine Red and Fire Orange

This stage is a final chance to tidy up before adding the last details to the miniature. Use a fine brush to apply black paint over any messy areas; this can be done at any stage if you feel the model needs it, the black picking up the undercoat and acting as an eraser for any of the other colours. You do need a steady hand when painting figures, but everyone makes mistakes, so it's good to know that it's easy enough to erase those mistakes when it's needed.

STEP 10: Skin mid-tones and other details.

STEP 11: Tidying up and piping details.

Add the final highlight to the Zouave jacket by mixing Carmine Red with a little Fire Orange, applying it in a dotted line in the same way as to the fez band. This allows some of the original Gory Red layer to show through here and there, and gives a good impression of the material moving as the soldier is charging.

## Step 12: Final details
*Colours:* Light Flesh, Brown Rose, Saddle Brown and White

This is the final stage when all the fine details are added, such as lips and hair shading. The final highlight on skin tone is also added at this point, using Light Flesh. These are perhaps the hardest parts of a miniature to paint, but painted well can bring the model to life by adding character to it. Eyes in particular are a defining feature, and must be added with a delicate touch with the best brush possible and a very steady hand.

If you find it difficult to add defined small eyes then they are best left as a brown line for the eye slit: the figure will look as if he is squinting, but this is preferable to him having massive eyes or looking in two directions at once! Add the eyes by placing two tiny white dots at each end of each eye slit; the brown line that was applied earlier in the eye slit then forms a brown dot in the middle, giving the appearance of a pupil.

Next paint the lips with Brown Rose, and finally the highlights for the hair. This figure has brown hair, so you can use the undercoat of black as the base coat, and just paint brown lines on the raised areas to create the highlights. Saddle Brown works well for this, as it is just bright enough to notice, without there being too much of a contrast between shades.

STEP 12: The final details are completed.

The finished Zouave miniature varnished and based.

These type of MDF bases are available from East Riding Miniatures. These bases are ideal for wargames miniatures.

## EXAMPLES OF LAYER PAINTING

The fabulous uniform of a Zouave suits the layer painting style well, because it is so elaborate. This style of painting offers a very clean-looking miniature with clearly defined colours, so it is ideal for parade uniforms and models with elaborate uniforms. In Chapter 8, which discusses basing, I will cover ideas and techniques on adding realism, and will demonstrate ways to reduce the clean appearance of your miniatures that layer painting gives, and give them a more weathered, 'campaign' look, without spoiling the paint you have lavished on them. At first it can seem heartbreaking to add mud, dirt and blood to a figure that you have slaved over for hours, but a little of this realism applied in the correct way really can add a great effect to some miniatures.

### Wheat's Tigers

This figure shows a member of the famous Zouave unit, known as the Tiger Rifles. This company was part of a special battalion commanded by Major Wheat, in the Louisiana Brigade, which was part of the Army of Northern Virginia. One of the most distinctive parts of this unit was the blue and white-striped ticking Zouave trousers. This was one of my reasons for showing this model. Painting a figure like this will not be for everyone, but with a bit of patience, a delicate touch and a good brush anything is possible.

The same layering technique mentioned previously was used to paint this figure, with a few additional details added. The white of the trousers was painted first using a mix of Tan Earth and Bone White for the first shade, then Bone White for the second shade and finally white for the highlight shade. The stripes were painted using a very fine brush, and any mistakes were tidied up using Bone White to keep the lines as straight as possible. I used Stormy Blue to create the stripes, painting one thick stripe and then two really fine ones in between. The one fortunate part of painting the Tiger Rifles is that it was only a company, so you only need a few. The rest of the battalion wore normal Confederate uniform.

### Duryee's Zouaves

This regiment was painted using the layer technique. The figures have three shades of each colour, giving a base tone, mid-tone and highlight. More could be applied, but three gives a good, rich effect, which

A Louisiana Tiger Zouave front view (*left*) and back view (*right*).
PAINTED BY STEVE BARBER.

is ideally suited to the flamboyant uniform of the Zouaves. Duryee's 5th New York Zouaves was one of the best disciplined regiments during the American Civil War. They were also one of the hardest fought. They saw action in numerous battles and sustained considerable casualties in the campaigns they were involved in.

The gorgeous uniform of all the Zouaves are enjoyable to paint, and they will light up your wargames table.

Duryee's 5th NYSM regiment.
28MM MINIATURES PAINTED BY STEVE BARBER.

# Painting with Washes 3

## INTRODUCTION TO PAINTING WITH WASHES

Using colour washes is a much quicker and simpler way to paint miniatures than using the layer painting technique. Because this method saves time it makes it ideal for painting the large numbers of figures needed to recreate large American Civil War armies. Quicker painting makes refighting the major battles such as Gettysburg more realistic for the majority of us whose time is limited to evenings and weekends.

The washes used for this style of painting are essentially a very watered-down paint. Because the paint is thinned, when it dries it is not opaque, allowing the colour underneath it to still show through. The base colour can be changed in a way that you decide, either in a subtle way, or not, depending how much water you add to the wash. Different colour washes can also be mixed together to create new colours, to help achieve the result you are seeking.

The wash style of painting is not about the details of an individual model, much as that is enjoyable to see, but the effect of a group of figures together. It is harder to control how the wash dries, making it less neat than the layer technique, which is all about neatness and style. Miniatures can be painted much faster using washes whilst still retaining a decent effect, which is why this style of painting is widely used amongst wargamers.

For those who prefer the layer painting method, it is possible to mix the techniques of layers with washes to create a very pleasing combination method of painting (as described in the next chapter). I use this combined method a lot when painting figures for my own collection. Indeed, many of the figures seen in the big scene photographs used throughout this book were painted using this technique.

Most of the paints used are the same as for the layer style of painting, the exception being the selection of washes required. The models are also prepared and undercoated in the same way. In this book I have used Vallejo washes to complement their paints. I have often used their washes over the years. There is a very good range available from the company, though for painting American Civil War miniatures only a few are normally required. The most widely used for any figures, regardless of the era, are black and burnt umber. These give the best shadows as they are dark, and they work well on a range of colours. The choice of wash for faces and hands is a personal preference – it all depends how dark you prefer the shading on your figures. If a greater contrast is required, then a darker wash can be applied.

This Confederate infantryman model was sprayed grey for the undercoat, and in this case the particular grey used was a widely available car primer spray paint. This was for two reasons. The first is that as a Confederate, the grey uniform is already painted so there is no need to paint trousers or jacket unless you want them to be a different colour, such as butternut brown. This helps speed up the painting process considerably.

The second reason is that as the miniature is going to be washed with darker colours to bring out the detail, the lighter the undercoat, the brighter the finished model will look. It makes some sense and saves some time if the main colour of the figure can be used as an undercoat, especially if jacket and trousers are the same colour.

All the base colours used in painting this miniature were squeezed on to a mixing tile; they have to be used in this way as the Vallejo paints come in a dropper bottle, rather than a pot with a lid. When painting on the base colours try to be as neat as possible, although areas of colour don't have to join entirely. If there is a small amount of the undercoat showing through between areas, or untidy lines, these can often be hidden when the washes are applied later. So you needn't worry too much about neatness at this stage.

The washes used can be thinned for a more delicate finish just by adding a little tap water to the painting tile with a size 2 brush or similar, and mixed until the desired consistency is reached. Rather than pour water on to the tile, it is best to drip the water from a paintbrush on to the tile, as you will have more control over how thin the wash will become. Thinning a wash like this for certain areas of the figure can achieve a good result; it will give more variation of tone, and in general will make the figure look less dark.

Paint washes dry fairly fast, as the high water content in them evaporates quickly. So it's best to use roughly the amount of wash you require and then pour out some more for the next figures, otherwise it will dry up by the time you are ready to paint them.

## PAINTING A 28MM CONFEDERATE INFANTRYMAN

The Confederate army was made up of troops from eleven different states, all of differing wealth; some states were therefore better able to resupply their regiments on campaign than others. Clothing quickly wore out in the field, and troops often had to forage what they could from the dead of both sides. Shoes were sometimes very poorly made by corrupt contractors and lasted no time at all.

As a result the Confederate infantryman soon came to have a less uniform look than may have been intended. The initial grey uniform was frequently replaced with captured Union clothes, which were sometimes re-dyed using homemade brown dyes. These greys and browns suit the wash-painting

method very well, and as you will see in the following steps, painting with washes is a lot simpler than layer painting. So when painting a Confederate figure you should decide which browns and greys you intend to use on the miniature before you start painting.

First, clean up the model by filing off the casting nub on the bottom of the base of the figure. Then scrape off any mould lines from the separate parts of the figure using a scalpel. Always take care when doing this, and scrape away from yourself when preparing the figure. These miniatures are from Steve Barber Models, and need to be glued together using superglue. I use Loctite Precision, which is strong and is ideal for this purpose.

Once your chosen miniature is cleaned up and glued together, glue it on a pot or on the end of a piece of dowel using a small amount of superglue; it is then ready to be undercoated.

For more information on preparing your figures, *see* Chapter 1 on preparation.

### Step 1: Undercoating
*Colours:* Grey primer spray paint

The first stage of the process is to undercoat the model. This will help the later layers of paint adhere to the metal miniature. The chosen colour of undercoat also helps to influence the overall finished effect of the miniature. For wash painting I prefer to use lighter colours on the main colour of the uniform, in this case grey for the Confederate uniform. Car spray paint in a matt grey primer is good for this, as it covers well in a smooth layer and is cost effective. Spraying is also a fast way of undercoating a large number of figures at once.

Always use spray paint outside because of the fumes. When spraying, if you group the models

STEP 1: Undercoating with grey primer.

STEP 2: Adding the clothing colours.

close together on newspaper this minimizes waste paint and will make the can last longer. Spray one side at a time, leaving a good ten minutes before turning them over to paint the other side. It may take a couple of coats on each side to give a good even coat. Try not to use too much paint at once, as painting in thin layers gives the best result.

## Step 2: Clothing
*Colours:* Tan Earth and Dark Grey

The uniform of a Confederate soldier was usually supposed to be grey. This often varied in shade between regiments and even companies, and was often replaced with whatever they could find at the time. For this miniature, I left the jacket the same grey as that used to undercoat the figure. Using the undercoat like this helps to speed up the painting process considerably. To give a bit of variety and to add some different tones to this figure, paint the trousers with Tan Earth and the hat with Dark Grey. Paint these base shades fairly neatly without worrying about getting really close to where that

particular colour will join up to another colour – for example, a strap.

## Step 3: The musket
*Colours:* Beige Brown

Paint the musket using Beige Brown. This brown is paler than you might think you would use, but it will be darkened by the application of washes later on. At this stage you only need paint the woodwork parts of the weapon. This leaves the grey undercoat showing through where the metallic silver will be painted later on. Although it's a good idea to be as neat as possible when painting in general, when using this method it isn't essential, as you will blend all the colours when you apply the washes further on in the process.

## Step 4: Equipment stage 1
*Colours:* Dark Grey and Flat Brown

Confederate equipment could be either black and brown leather, or a mixture of the two. Paint the belts in Dark Grey first, being careful not to get any of the dark colour on the lighter grey jacket. Then paint the

STEP 3: Painting the musket with Beige Brown.

STEP 4: Equipment stage 1.

STEP 5: Equipment stage 2.

cap pouch on the front of the miniature's belt in Dark Grey, and his shoes using Flat Brown. Alternatively paint them in Dark Grey to achieve black shoes, which they also used. Paint the cartridge box on the back of the model using Flat Brown. These colours could easily be swapped round, or just the one colour used if you prefer a more uniformed look.

### Step 5: Equipment stage 2
*Colours:* Bone White and Tan Earth

The equipment is mostly finished at this stage; there is just the water bottle and haversack to do. Paint the haversack using Bone White: this is a good colour for natural linen, which they were often made from. Paint the haversack strap in Bone White too. Once again, take your time painting the straps, as it is easy to get the white on the grey jacket accidentally, and you will then have to paint over the mistakes with grey – so a little time spent at this stage will save time later.

Paint the water bottle and strap using Tan Earth. The water-bottle strap is very thin, so you will need a good fine brush to paint this without spilling any paint on the surrounding areas.

STEP 6: Adding the metallics.

STEP 7: Painting the skin tones using Basic Skin Tone.

## Step 6: Metallics

*Colours:* Gold and Silver

You need to paint a few small areas in this step. First paint the belt buckles using Vallejo Gold, then the end of the bayonet scabbard in the same colour, and also the few visible buttons on the jacket front and cuffs. After painting all the gold areas, next start painting the musket barrel, stock plate, lock and trigger with Vallejo Silver. A few tiny areas can easily be missed, such as the musket-strap clip edges where the strap joins the musket, so make sure to paint these silver.

The last parts in this step to paint are the top of the water bottle, and the three tiny clips that hold the strap on the water bottle. Paint these silver too.

## Step 7: Skin

*Colours:* Basic Skin Tone

Next paint the visible flesh areas with Vallejo Basic Skin Tone. On this miniature only the hands, face and ears are visible, so there isn't a lot to do. Paint around the hair and beard line on the model fairly neatly. It isn't essential to avoid painting on areas that will have colour applied later, but the

more layers of paint that are added to an area, the less well the washes will work. This is because the recessed areas on the figure will fill up with paint and then the wash has nowhere to sink into.

You will need a steady hand and a fine brush to paint under the hat and around the fingers on the right hand. Details such as this, even when using the washes technique, make all the difference to the finished miniature.

## Step 8: Hair and details

*Colours:* Leather Brown

Now you can see the miniature is starting to look the part. The last area of the figure to which you apply the main colour is the hair and the beard. Of course you can paint these in any hair colour, but I chose Leather Brown. Apply the paint with a fine brush; once again a steady hand is required when painting around the hat and the face in particular. Although washes cover quite a lot, you don't want to get spots of dark colour on the flesh tones.

Once these areas are painted the figure is finished in its basic form. Only the application of the washes now remains.

STEP 8: Adding hair and other details.

STEP 9: Applying washes to the clothing.

STEP 10: Applying washes to some of the equipment.

### Step 9: Washes for clothing

*Colours:* Dark Grey wash and Brown wash

Apply a Vallejo Dark Grey wash to the figure's jacket, taking care not to get the wash on other areas. Then apply the brown wash quite liberally to the trousers. Both of these washes will considerably change the tone of the figure. The jacket comes out a darker grey this way, but if you prefer a lighter grey finish then paint the jacket a very light grey at Step 2 when you paint the rest of the clothing. When painting a regiment, this variation in grey can make the finished unit look more interesting and realistic, so it is well worth the extra time and effort to paint some light grey coats or trousers.

### Step 10: Washes for some of the equipment

*Colours:* Black wash

Carefully apply a black wash over the grey belts and gold buckles of the figure, using enough wash to spill slightly over the sides of the belts. This over-spill helps to add a shadow border to certain detail items that you want to stand out. The black wash also really helps define the details of the gold buckles themselves. Continue this wash application over the bayonet scabbard, shoes and hat; once the black wash has been applied to the dark grey of the hat and belts it gives the impression that the belts are black with grey highlights.

After these two washes have been added, it is then possible to see what the figure will look like once it is finished.

### Step 11: Washes for skin

*Colours:* Brown wash

This step is a simple one but really adds character to the model. Apply the brown wash quite liberally to the face and hands of the miniature. Areas of flesh should still be seen through the wash when applied, but there should be enough to pool in the eyes and deeper recesses. Apply the same amount of wash to the hands, allowing it to sink into the gaps between the fingers, which helps greatly in giving them definition.

The choice of wash colour for flesh areas is a personal one. Vallejo produce a flesh-coloured wash, but I prefer their brown wash for flesh tones as the darker colour gives greater definition to the finished model. Most of the time figures are not examined closely, but are seen at arm's length as they are moved across a wargames' table. If you prefer the redness of the flesh wash, the brown and the flesh could always be mixed together to create a more earthy tone.

### Step 12: Final washes

*Colours:* Black wash and Burnt Umber wash

So the miniature is almost finished now. Mix some Black wash and Burnt Umber wash together in equal amounts, and apply this mix to the water bottle to create a darker, more contrasting shade of brown. Then apply Burnt Umber wash to the haversack and strap, and the water-bottle strap. Apply Black wash to the water-bottle opening, and finally to the hair and beard. Because of the dark shade of brown used for the hair, the Black wash only creates a small amount of contrast. To create more contrasting hair you can just use a lighter brown or blonde base shade and wash it with either Black wash or Burnt Umber wash. This will give a much greater and more noticeable contrast for the hair and beard.

STEP 11: Applying a brown wash to the skin areas.

STEP 12a: Applying the final washes.

River skirmish.

## PAINTING A 10MM CONFEDERATE INFANTRYMAN

The following step-by-step painting of a 10mm miniature demonstrates the similarities and differences of painting smaller scale models. The example shown is an unreleased 10mm American Civil War miniature from Steve Barber Models. He is wearing a kepi, so could equally be painted as a Union infantryman, but the Confederates also wore kepis so I chose to paint him in grey. Figures of this size are better painted in batches of ten or twenty, but for the purposes of this demonstration we are just concentrating on painting one miniature.

### Step 1: Undercoating

*Colours:* Grey primer spray paint

10mm miniatures need undercoating for all the same reasons as we have covered before, but take care with figures of this size so as not to clog up the details with too much paint. As the model is smaller, grey primer spray paint is perfect for giving an even coverage, and as it is lighter this will help the colours show up more, even for Union troops.

Always use spray paint outside because of the fumes. When spraying, group the figures as closely

STEP 12b: The finished 28mm
Confederate infantryman.

STEP 1: Undercoating
with grey spray primer.

STEP 2: Clothing.

STEP 3: Painting the musket.

together as possible on newspaper in order to minimize wasting paint. It may take several coats on each side to give a good even covering. Leave about ten minutes between coats. Try not to use too much paint at once as painting in thin layers gives the best result, especially on smaller miniatures.

### Step 2: Clothing

*Colours:* Silver Grey, Dark Grey, Beige Brown

You could leave all the figure's clothing in the grey primer that was used for his undercoat, but in this case paint his jacket and kepi Silver Grey. Take care to paint round his straps and equipment. Then paint the peak of his kepi and his shoes with Dark Grey. Lastly paint his trousers using Beige Brown. Take as much care as possible to get close to the next colour, such as where his jacket meets his trousers – though as before, once the washes are applied they will hide most of these joins.

### Step 3: Musket

*Colours:* Beige Brown and Dark Grey

At this scale woodgrain is irrelevant, so the woodwork areas of the musket need only one coat. Use Beige Brown to paint this area, as this is a nice

mid-coloured brown. The colour will of course be darker once the washes are applied. Take care to avoid getting brown on the metal areas of the musket, such as the barrel and bayonet. Once you have completed the woodwork areas, paint the musket strap Dark Grey. The remaining parts of the musket are metallics and will be painted in Steps 5 and 6.

### Step 4: Equipment

*Colours:* Dark Grey and Beige Brown

Confederate equipment could be either black or brown leather, so you have a choice as to how you want the miniature to turn out. For this figure I chose to make it mostly black, and only painted the water bottle a different colour. Paint the belts, cartridge box, bayonet scabbard and haversack in Dark Grey, and the water-bottle strap with a fine brush in Beige Brown. Both these colours will darken once the washes are applied in a later stage, when they will look like black and brown leather.

### Step 5: Metallics

*Colours:* Silver and Gold

There isn't much metalwork to paint on this figure. Use silver to paint the metal parts of the musket, such

STEP 4: Painting the equipment.

STEP 5: Painting the metallic areas.

STEP 6: Painting the face, hands and hair.

STEP 7: Adding the flesh wash first.

as the barrel, hoops, bayonet and butt plate. As the miniature is smaller, a brighter colour than Oily Steel is needed in order to make the metal more discernible after applying the washes. The water bottle is also a type of metal so paint this in silver too. Use gold to paint the few tiny buckles on the figure's belts and the couple of buttons on his jacket, and lastly the two tiny buttons on the sides of his kepi.

### Step 6: Face, hands and hair
*Colours:* Basic Skin Tone, Beige Brown, Gold and Silver

Paint the figure's hands and face using Basic Skin Tone, then his hair and moustache using Beige Brown. The moustache is tiny so you will need to be patient when painting it!

At this stage I noticed that I had missed a couple of metallic details so I painted them at this stage, the tiny end of the bayonet scabbard using Vallejo Gold paint and the butt plate of the musket in Silver. 10mm figures are rarely painted one at a time and are easier to paint as a production line, where all the metallic areas are painted at once. This is useful on small figures where details can be easily missed, because if you miss it on one, the chances are that you will notice it on one of the others.

### Step 7: Flesh wash
*Colours:* Brown wash

This stage is very quick and easy. Paint the figure's hands and face liberally with Brown wash; this will sink nicely into all the details of the hands and face and reveal details such as the eyes, which were previously difficult to see. The wash also covers the join of his cuffs with his hands. I also applied it to his hair to see if it was dark enough, but it wasn't quite, so covered his hair with the main wash during the next step.

### Step 8: Main wash
*Colours:* Dark Grey

Once again, this is an easy step. Paint all the rest of the areas of the model liberally with a Dark Grey wash. This will sink into all the recesses and reveal all the details on the figure. The Dark Grey will also darken some of the colours that were previously quite pale.

Figures of this scale can be painted on a strip of wood, which is slim enough to get good grip on; in this way you can apply all the washes to one figure

STEP 8: Applying the main wash to finish the figure.

after another in a production line. This is a very fast way of painting, and there is no reason that a whole regiment can't be painted at once.

## EXAMPLE OF A MINIATURE PAINTED WITH WASHES

### Confederate Artillery Crew

The uniforms for the Confederate artillery crew shown here are quite simple and ideally suited to being painted using washes. Initially they were all sprayed grey using the car primer, in the same way as the Confederate infantry figures in those step-by-step sections. The artillery crew were painted using Vallejo paints and washes.

ABOVE: A 28mm Confederate 12pdr artillery piece in action. *PAINTED BY STEVE BARBER.*

BELOW: A 28mm Confederate Parrott rifled cannon in action. *PAINTED BY STEVE BARBER.*

# INTRODUCING COMBINATION PAINTING

The wash method of painting demonstrated in the previous chapter is not to everyone's tastes. Equally, not everyone is capable of achieving the very neat results needed for layer painting, no matter how much they would like to. Layer painting also takes quite a lot longer to do than the wash technique. With those things in mind I combined the two methods to come up with a combination technique. The idea of this is that the detail of layer painting can be combined with the speed of painting with washes, in the hope that this will allow you to paint your troops to a high standard more quickly than the traditional layer painting method allows, but

still enabling you to create decent sized armies in a reasonable time frame.

Quite a few of the figures in this book have been painted with this combination technique: it is easy to learn and offers professional results quickly.

There is no doubt that paint washes suit certain areas of a miniature better than others. Of course, in time when painting your own figures you may decide differently. Everyone has different tastes and expectations when it comes to painting, as with most things in life.

Besides general use on painting clothing, washes can also be used to help to blend colours on larger areas, as well as adding interesting effects to a figure. Some painters use them very sparingly, while others will dip the whole figure in, colouring a whole

Confederate reinforcements arrive on the battlefield.

*MODEL BUILDINGS BY HOVELS AND SARRISSA PRECISION, FLAGS BY FLAGS OF WAR AND GMB DESIGNS.*
*THE MINIATURES ARE PAINTED BY STEVE BARBER. THE MODEL TREES ARE SUPPLIED BY THE MODEL TREE SHOP.*

The battlefield from the air.

The 5th New Hampshire, led by Colonel Cross, fire a volley at the advancing foe.

*FLAGS BY GMB DESIGNS. PAINTED BY STEVE BARBER. MODEL TREES BY THE MODEL TREE SHOP.*

model in a single colour wash. Basically it comes down to where you think washes are best applied on the figure you are working on. To my mind they work well on clothing most of the time, and less well on faces and flesh areas. In the end, though, it is your choice as to how you use them, and where you think they save you painting time and give you the result you were trying to achieve.

## PAINTING A UNION INFANTRYMAN USING COMBINATION PAINTING

The Union army usually had a more uniformed look that the Confederates due to the industrial power of the northern states. Most regiments were equipped with the same clothing of a dark blue jacket and kersey or sky blue trousers. This makes the Union army much simpler to paint, as they can be painted in a 'production line' way, more easily than the Confederates can be. That said, there is much more room for creativity when painting the Confederate army. The choice of greys and browns certainly requires more thought than a Union army would do.

STEP 1: Undercoating using black primer.

Many of the Union miniatures featured in this book were painted using the combination technique. I feel it works especially well on these, and allows for regiments to be painted reasonably fast, whilst still giving them an attractive detailed finish.

### Step 1: Undercoating
*Colours:* Black spray primer

The first stage is to undercoat the model. Just as with layer painting, combination painting also has a black undercoat. This undercoat helps the later layers of paint to adhere to the metal figure. Matt black car spray paint is good for this as it covers well in a smooth layer and is cost effective. Spraying is also a fast way of undercoating a large number of figures at once.

Always use spray paint outside because of the fumes, which can be dangerous if inhaled. When spraying, group the miniatures as closely as possible together on newspaper in order to minimize wasting paint. Spray one side at a time, leaving ten minutes or so before turning the figures over to paint the other side. It will take a couple of coats on each side to give a good, even coat, which is essential if we are to preserve as much detail as possible on the miniatures. Resist the urge to try and get them undercoated as fast as possible as too much paint at once will cause details to be lost under gloopy paint and will spoil the miniature.

### Step 2: Base shades for the clothing
*Colours:* Stormy Blue and Deep Sky Blue

Use Stormy Blue as the base shade for the jacket of this Union figure. This dark blue colour will become even darker with the addition of a black wash later on. Take care when painting round the straps and belts that go over the jacket. Also paint the cloth parts of the kepi in Stormy Blue; this leaves the peak, strap and buttons of the kepi still in black. Then paint the model's kersey blue trousers using Deep Sky Blue, taking care where his two legs join to leave a fine black line still visible, which helps to define the legs on the finished miniature.

The uniformity of Union armies means that the choice of colours available for us to use for this figure's clothing is limited to just the light and dark blue. Even so, they are attractive colours, and the Vallejo paints are a joy to paint with.

STEP 2: Painting the base shades for the clothing.

STEP 3: Adding the musket woodwork and grain.

## Step 3: Musket woodwork and grain

*Colours:* Flat Brown, Tan Earth and Beige Brown

Paint the base shade for the musket's woodwork using Flat Brown. This is quite intricate painting, so you will need a fine brush, and to take care when

STEP 4: Adding the clothing layers.

painting around the musket hoops and other metalwork areas. Then mix some Tan Earth and Beige Brown together on the mixing tile, and paint fine lines on the wood areas horizontally along the gun to represent grain lines. As this musket will be washed, use a lighter grain than before to make sure it is still visible after the wash has been added. The lightness of the grain is personal choice, and just helps to indicate the difference of materials used on the weapon.

At this stage paint the top and sides of the water-bottle cover using some of the Deep Sky Blue already on the mixing tile from the previous step.

## Step 4: Clothing layers

*Colours:* Stormy Blue, Light Blue and Light Grey

Using the layering technique, apply Sky Blue to the raised areas on the trousers; this brings out the details on the material nicely. Also paint a few diagonal stripes in Sky Blue across the water-bottle cover, to give it some texture. Then mix some Light Grey into some Stormy Blue on the mixing tile for the highlights on the jacket and kepi. Make this lighter than you would normally as these areas will have a wash applied to them.

As a result of using the wash stage only one highlight is used on the clothing, as opposed to the two used in the layering technique. This means there is no need to paint one of the layers that would normally be painted using the layer technique – which in turn means that not having to paint one of the more time-consuming layer stages makes this method much faster when painting regiments and larger groups of figures. The few minutes saved per figure on every layer saves an hour or more when painting each regiment.

### Step 5: Metallics

*Colours:* Gold, Silver and Black

A number of small gold details need to be painted using Vallejo Gold, from buttons to the cartridge-box badge and bayonet scabbard tip. It is important to take time over this stage to make sure nothing is missed, as this is easy to do. Next paint the silver details: three small silver loops on the water bottle and the water-bottle lid, then the metalwork on the musket.

It was at this stage that I noticed there was a messy bit of Light Blue that had got on to the black of one of the figure's shoes, so I corrected this with some black paint. I prefer to tidy up as I go along,

rather than leaving it all to the end, as I don't like looking at messy areas whilst I'm painting.

### Step 6: Equipment shading

*Colours:* Dark Grey, London Grey and Bone White

For the shading colour for the black areas, such as the shoes and all the straps and equipment except the water-bottle strap, mix Dark Grey with some London Grey. Avoid properly mixing the two colours as this gives variation when applying the paint. The equipment used by the Union was mostly black, so it is very quick to paint when a black undercoat is used.

The water-bottle strap is the only part still to be painted after the grey highlights have been added. You will need a very fine brush, as it is a very thin strap. Use Bone White for this task. Only one shade is required, and this thin cream strap does make the miniature pop out more.

### Step 7: Flesh base shades

*Colours:* Flat Flesh

This is a simpler stage to do, as only one colour of paint is required. Use Flat Flesh as the base shade for the flesh parts of this model; as a wash will be

STEP 5: Painting the metallic details.

STEP 6: Shading the equipment.

applied later you don't want it to be too dark a colour to start with. Only the figure's hands and face need to be painted flesh, so it is quick to do. Take care around the hands and fingers, and use a very fine brush to paint the tip of the trigger finger, which is just visible behind the gun.

Then paint the ears, neck and face using Flat Flesh. Don't worry too much about accuracy on the face, and it doesn't have to be too neat round the beard, as this will be painted over in a later stage. But there is something about adding the flesh areas to a miniature that immediately brings it to life!

## Step 8: Flesh layers

*Colours:* Light Flesh

This is another simple step, with only one colour required. In order to paint the layers on the flesh tones you will need a really good fine brush, preferably at least a size 0. The most important factor with brushes is the point, so a size 1 with a really good point might also do the job well, but ideally use a size 0. As the flesh tones are going to be washed brown, the highlights on the flesh need to be very light, so use Vallejo Light Flesh for this task.

Apply a few stripes on the exposed part of the figure's neck, then paint dabs on the raised areas of his face. Next paint the knuckles, and then the fingers and the tendons on his hands. Once again apply a small dab of paint to the exposed part of his trigger finger behind the musket. This is quite a difficult detail to get at with a paintbrush, so you will need a steady hand and some patience.

## Step 9: Hair and other details

*Colours:* Beige Brown and Brown Rose

Paint the miniature's hair and beard using Beige Brown. Try not to get any of the brown on the flesh parts that have just been painted. It is quite tricky getting to some areas of his beard where it's near the musket, so take your time with this. The figure is looking finished by this stage and could be left just like this if you wanted to, but the series of washes that follow help to add definition to the figure, and tone down some of the colours that have been used.

Also during this stage paint his lips using Brown Rose from Vallejo. Painting the lips is only a tiny detail to add and isn't essential, especially as he has a beard, so you don't have to do this if you don't

STEP 7: Painting the base shade using Flat Flesh.

STEP 8: Adding the flesh layers.

STEP 9: Painting the hair and other details.

STEP 10: Applying the black wash.

want to. However, I like to add details to the figure's face to help bring him to life as much as possible.

## Step 10: Clothing washes

*Colours:* Black wash

Black wash was applied fairly liberally all over the jacket. It is important not to do this too thinly as it will just smear over the clothing. It would also be incorrect to apply so much wash that it runs off the model. To achieve the desired effect apply just enough to sink into all the recesses.

Take care to paint this wash up to the cream water-bottle strap and not over it. This helps to define the strap even more, though this isn't essential. At this stage the lid of the water bottle and the figure's shoes were also painted with black wash.

Next apply a watered-down brown wash fairly liberally over the figure's trousers. The purpose of watering it down is to dull the blue colours slightly and muddy them, rather than allowing the wash to sink into all the recesses and cover the base shade completely.

## Step 11: Equipment, flesh and musket washes

*Colours:* Black wash, Brown wash and Burnt Umber

Much of the figure's straps and equipment had washes applied to them during the previous stage, so only the water bottle remains to be finished. The best colour for this task is Burnt Umber, as it is less harsh than black; the natural dark brown helps to muddy

STEP 11: Painting a wash over the equipment, musket and flesh.

STEP 12: Adding the final highlights to complete the miniature.

the water bottle slightly. So carefully apply Burnt Umber wash from Vallejo to just the water bottle.

Next, wash the flesh areas of the miniature using a brown wash. Apply it fairly liberally so that it sinks into all the creases of his face and hands. Then paint the musket with a black wash, again applying it fairly liberally. At this point also apply black wash to his hair and beard: this helps to dull down the colour of his hair and to give it definition and shading. Apply the wash quite carefully around his beard to avoid getting it on his face.

### Step 12: Final highlights

*Colours:* Gold, Tan Earth

I hope that by this stage you are very satisfied with your almost finished model, but now is the chance to tweak anything that you are not quite happy with. It is an opportunity for the figure to have just a little more attention lavished on it. This is not essential, and you may be entirely happy with the result already, but depending on the type of figure a few little extra highlights on his face, as I did here, will help the miniature to stand out a bit more. A few of the gold details had become too dark for my taste after the washes had been added, so I went over the

belt buckle and the bayonet scabbard tip with some gold paint to brighten them up. If the washes left any messy marks on the figure, then you can also tidy these up at this point.

I felt with this model that the hair and beard needed a bit more definition to make them more discernible, so I added some highlights using Tan Earth.

## SUMMARY

The idea of this chapter is to demonstrate that by combining painting styles it is possible to achieve a great result and save some time into the bargain. This version of the combination painting technique was how I painted the majority of my own 28mm American Civil War collection. I wanted to paint bigger regiments, and knew that I wouldn't have the time to paint them using layering, but I also wanted them to be figures that I would be proud to display in my collection. I really like the grubbiness that the washes add to the models. This makes them more realistic and less bright than if I had just used layer painting. I like the 'campaign' look for my Civil War troops, so a certain amount of grubbiness works well for me. So I tried out mixing the two techniques and set about painting both my armies.

The step-by-step example of combination painting in this chapter combines the layer painting and wash techniques, but it could equally be a combination of other painting methods, such as blending wet layers and using targeted washes in certain areas for particular effects. Layer and dry-brushing techniques can be combined, as can washes and dry brushing. It is important to make sure the wash layers are properly dry before any dry brushing is done to avoid smearing the paint. All the techniques could even be used together on the same miniature if you thought it would benefit it.

There is no particular order in which the washes should be used. During this process of combining washes and layering it doesn't matter which order you use them in, or how you do so. They can be used first, last or anywhere in between – it is entirely down to your own creativity and what you feel best suits the miniature that you are working on.

It is also really up to you how much or how little you do to the figure you are painting. If painting armies quickly is your goal, then using washes is undeniably the best method for you. If you want to paint to collect, then it is worth perfecting painting with layers, as this will give you the nicest result for your collection – but the down side is that the armies will take time to build up. But why not experiment with painting styles and try out your own version of the combination technique?

# EXAMPLES OF COMBINATION PAINTING

## 1st Texas Regiment

This regiment of thirty figures was painted using the combination painting technique. The models were sprayed with grey primer spray paint to start with, as that was the main colour of the Confederate uniform. The base shade on a few of the miniatures was then altered to add some variety to the regiment. The clothing had a second layer painted over the base shade, as you would do in the layering style.

The clothing areas were then washed with a dark grey for the grey items, and either brown or burnt umber for the butternut brown jackets and trousers. Flesh tones were painted with just a single colour, and washed with a brown wash. Muskets and equipment were washed with a black wash.

The figures were based on rectangle MDF bases from East Riding Miniatures. Scenic tufts and static grass were added to the bases to add the finishing touch.

## Tennessee Thompson

Private Thompson was a soldier in the 1st Tennessee Regiment who became noted for the amount of equipment he carried with him. For most soldiers there was a certain amount of carrying what you owned, but clearly Private Thompson took this a degree further.

The 1st Texas Regiment marching.

*FLAGS ARE BY FLAGS OF WAR. MINIATURES PAINTED BY STEVE BARBER.*

The model took a bit of assembling before he could be painted. All the parts were glued together with Loctite superglue. He was painted using the combination technique, but a number of layers were applied before washes were used. He was based on a round MDF base from East Riding Miniatures. When the filler was applied to the base, indents were made using a modelling tool. Once this had dried and been painted, gloss varnish was dripped into the indents to form puddles on the road he was trudging through.

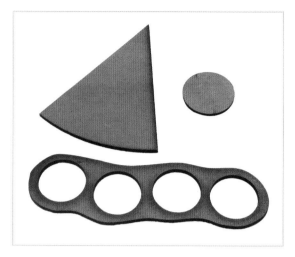

A selection of some of the many shapes and sizes of MDF bases available from East Riding Miniatures.

## The Grenade Thrower

It is probably not widely known, but small numbers of hand grenades were used during the American Civil War. These primitive grenades were very hazardous to use, and in one case were actually caught in blankets by resourceful defenders and thrown back against their attackers. This miniature of a Union infantryman is throwing one of these early grenades.

The figure has been painted using the combination technique. He has had a black wash applied to his jacket and a watered-down brown wash to his trousers. His trousers have had a second layer of sky blue painted on them before the wash

Tennessee Thompson – possibly the most encumbered soldier in the Confederate army!

A Union grenade thrower. The Civil War did see many inventions like this even though they saw limited use.

*PAINTED BY STEVE BARBER.*

A Union ammunition carrier.

*PAINTED BY STEVE BARBER.*

was applied. The musket was also washed using a black wash.

The figure's hands and face and many of the other details have all been painted with the layer technique.

He was then based on a round MDF base with a few small stones. This base was painted and dry brushed, and then a few grass tufts and a small amount of static grass were applied to it to finish the model.

## The Ammunition Carrier

This Union ammunition carrier was painted using the method described in the step-by-step demonstration in this chapter. The writing on the box of ammunition was painted using a very watery white paint and an extremely fine brush. When doing really fine writing or other details you need to be completely relaxed, and there is no point attempting it if you are not. Leave this part until you find the

right moment, otherwise it will probably go wrong. With peace and quiet and some patience, details like this are possible. Little extras like this can really make the model stand out, so if possible they are definitely worth adding when you can.

Once again this figure was based on a round MDF base from East Riding Miniatures. Paint and dry brush the base, and then for the final details I applied static grass, a broken tree branch from Steve Barber Models and a grass tuft.

## A Typical Base for Confederate Infantry

Most wargames figures are based in small groups. My own ACW miniatures are mostly based in groups of three. These miniatures were painted using the combination technique with a little extra fine detail work added to create the check shirt. Once again these miniatures are based on an MDF base from East Riding Miniatures and painted using Vallejo paints.

A typical Confederate base of three figures.

## INTRODUCTION TO PAINTING HORSES

There are, of course, a lot of breeds and colours of horse, but regiments of cavalry would often try to keep horses of the same colour either for different squadrons or for the whole regiment. During wartime, horses that were unsuitable through age, health or size were often drafted in to fill the ranks as casualties mounted. The main colours of horse that are needed for wargaming purposes are generally bay and chestnut, though there may be the occasional grey, black or palomino in amongst them. For the purposes of this book the next two step-by-step guides focus on the bay and chestnut horses that you will need.

The wash method and the dry-brushing method are shown separately here, but as with the artillery painting guides in the next chapter, they can be mixed to create a combination method in the same way as was demonstrated on the infantry figure. This can give a softer effect, as the washes will dull the dry-brushing strokes and help to blend the colours together. Both techniques are especially good at emphasizing the muscle areas of the horse. Creating some depth in the muscles helps to emphasize the power of a charging horse and gives movement to the miniatures.

Once you have chosen the technique you are going to use, and have decided whether you will be painting bay or chestnut horses, all that remains is to clean up the miniatures and get started. When cleaning up the horse models, make sure to remove the mould sprue underneath the base with a file so that the model stands up properly. Then go over the length of the horse, removing the mould line with a scalpel; take care as you do this. It is particularly important that the mould line is removed, as traces of this will really spoil the finished look of the miniature.

## PAINTING A BAY HORSE USING DRY BRUSHING

The bay horse should really be the most common type in your army. There are, however, quite a few colour shades, from pale to dark, that you can paint your bay horses, so they don't all have to look the same. This variety in colour is nice to paint and will prevent the horses from becoming boring to do. Variation such as this will really make your figures stand out from the crowd.

Bay horses could either have black manes and tails or cream colour manes and tails. So they don't all have to be black! Adding these details to your miniatures will make the finished regiments or gun teams look cool!

### Step 1: Undercoating
*Colours:* Black spray paint

As with all the previous painting projects, the process of painting a horse begins with undercoating.

STEP 1: Undercoating using black spray paint.

When spraying the model make sure the spray reaches under its belly and around the legs. Good coverage is important, especially when using the dry-brush technique, because any bare metal areas will definitely show through the dry brushing if the undercoat is not done properly. With both methods the undercoat helps the layers of paint show through and in this case acts as the base shade. I prefer to use spray as this method is fast, and it also gives a very even coating if several thin coats are applied.

## Step 2 – Base shade
*Colours:* Flat Brown

As this is going to be a bay horse, its legs, mane and tail need to be left black. This is the reason for undercoating the horse black. Flat Brown from Vallejo makes an ideal base coat for a bay horse. Drop a little of the colour on to the mixing tile, and using an old brush, dry brush the model lightly at first to leave areas of black showing through to create shadows. Also leave black the areas inside the legs and a little under the horse's belly. Once you have finished dry

STEP 2: Base shade.

STEP 3: Mid-tone dry brush.

brushing the base shade, tidy up the mane and tail using black paint and a fine brush.

### Step 3: Mid-tone dry brush
*Colours:* Flat Brown and Gold Brown

To create a mid-tone highlight, Flat Brown and some Gold Brown were mixed together. This mix was then dry brushed on the model. The top of the horse was not dry brushed to leave it the base brown, but instead the dry brushing was concentrated on the sides of the horse. A little extra dry brushing was applied to the sides of the horse's belly. Once again for photographic purposes the mane and tail were tidied up with black paint. Normally this would only need to be done at the final highlight stage.

### Step 4: Highlight dry brush
*Colours:* Flat Brown and Gold Brown

For the final highlight for this horse make a lighter mix of Flat Brown and Gold Brown, and dry brush this carefully over the sides of the horse, picking out the raised areas at the edges of the legs and the belly. Once this has been done it can look a bit stark so I usually lightly dry brush the base colour over the top of this highlight. It puts a bit of warmth back into the model, as the Flat Brown is quite a reddish-brown in colour. It also still allows the final highlight to show through without it becoming too dominating. However, variations in colour are a good thing when painting a unit, as you don't want all the horses to be exactly the same shade of bay, as that would not be realistic.

### Step 5: Mane, tail and legs mid-tone
*Colours:* Dark Grey

Next paint the mane, tail and lower legs. Pour a little Dark Grey on to the mixing tile for this. Dark Grey is an excellent first highlight colour for anything that is black, as it will help black things stand out more and allow the details in those areas to be seen more clearly.

Next dry brush the mane, tail and lower legs with Dark Grey. Do this carefully around the mane and the tail in particular so as not to get the Dark Grey on to the brown body. Dry brush the lower legs right to the base so that the hooves are covered as well.

### Step 6: Mane, tail and legs highlights
*Colours:* London Grey

Make the last highlight for the mane, tail and lower legs using London Grey. This colour is a little lighter than the Dark Grey, but not too different. Dry brush the London Grey very carefully to avoid getting any grey paint on the brown body of the horse. Also only apply it to the ends of the tail and mane, just lightening the ends of the horse's hair; this allows the Dark Grey still to be visible further up the tail and mane.

STEP 4: Highlight dry brush.

STEP 5: Adding the mid-tones
to the mane, tail and legs.

All the dry brushing was done using the same old bigger brush that I often use for dry brushing. It's always worth keeping old brushes!

## Step 7: Socks and hooves

*Colours:* Bone White, White, London Grey and Medium Grey

The first decision to make at this stage is which of the horse's feet best suit socks, if any. This can be affected by the previous stages, as to how brown or grey the legs are. The base colour for the socks is Bone White. Paint this neatly around the hooves, and in a more jagged line on the legs. Also paint a small stripe of Bone White on the horse's nose at this stage. Make the highlight for these areas using white, applying it in vertical stripes to enhance the jagged areas of the socks. Then paint the hooves using a mix of London Grey and Medium Grey. It doesn't matter if these colours aren't mixed properly as horses' hooves can have this varied mix of colours.

## Step 8: Eyes and details

*Colours:* Black, Flat Brown, Dark Grey and White

The horse is now almost complete. All that remains to paint are the last few details. First of all paint the eyes and the nostrils black, and the recess

STEP 6: Mane, tail
and legs highlight.

STEP 7: Painting the socks and hooves.

STEP 8: Painting the eyes and final details.

between the lips. Then mix together some Flat Brown and black for the eye colour, and apply it to the eyes: horses' eyes are a very dark brown. Next place a tiny dot of white at the back of each eye using a very fine brush. The eyes are now complete.

The final detail is the horse's nose. Dry brush the nose lightly using Dark Grey. Try to avoid getting any of the grey paint in the horse's nostrils. Once this has been painted the horse is complete!

## PAINTING A CHESTNUT HORSE USING WASHES

The chestnut horse colour was less common than the bay colour, but it should still feature amongst the ranks of figures that you paint. Whilst an attempt was sometimes made to place same colour horses within a squadron, this was mostly unrealistic and harked back to the Napoleonic wars when horses of the same colour in a unit was desired. But the carnage of these wars caused serious damage to the horse stocks of Europe, which took decades to recover.

## Step 1: Undercoating
*Colours:* Grey primer

As with all the previous miniatures, the process of painting a chestnut horse begins with undercoating. When spraying the model make sure the spray reaches under the belly of the horse and around the legs. Good coverage is important especially when using the dry-brush technique, as any bare metal areas will definitely show through the dry brushing if the undercoating is not done properly. With both methods the undercoat helps the next layers of

paint show through, and in this case acts as the base shade.

I prefer to use spray as it is a fast method, and it also gives a very even coating when done using several thin coats. As this horse is going to be painted using washes, which will darken the paint effect, undercoat the model with grey primer spray paint.

## Step 2: Base shade for the flesh
*Colours:* Cavalry Brown, Gold Brown and Flat Brown

Make an even mix of Cavalry Brown and Gold Brown on the mixing tile, then add a small amount of Flat Brown to darken the colour slightly. Apply this colour evenly over the body of the miniature, taking care to

STEP 1: Undercoating using grey spray primer.

STEP 2: Painting the base shade for the flesh.

avoid leaving areas of grey still showing in hard-to-reach areas, such as under the body and the insides of the legs. Leave the hooves, mane and tail grey. The reason for not painting these areas is that extra layers of paint will fill up the recesses on a model, which will make the washes that are applied later less effective.

### Step 3: The base shade for the mane and tail
*Colours:* Gold Brown, Cavalry Brown, Light Grey and Flat Brown

Mix together Cavalry Brown and a little Flat Brown on the mixing tile. Add to this a larger amount of Gold Brown to create a slightly lighter version of the body colour. Generally chestnut horses have manes and tails that are a very similar colour to their flesh, but in order to make these stand out a little more,

they can be painted in a slightly lighter or slightly darker version of the body colour. When painting the mane and tail avoid getting any of the different colour on the body of the horse.

Whilst the tail is still wet, paint a little light grey on to the wet tail at the bottom, and blend it up and down until you achieve a lighter end to the tail. Lightly dry brush the same colour over the mane.

Lastly paint the ears a mix of Cavalry Brown and Gold Brown to achieve a slightly different tone to the rest of the body.

### Step 4: Shading
*Colours:* Gold Brown and Cavalry Brown

To create an extra highlight to help accent some of the raised details on this model make a mix of

STEP 3: The base shade for the mane and tail.

STEP 4: Shading.

mainly Gold Brown with a tiny amount of Cavalry Brown added to it. Then lightly brush this all over the horse. It is a case of almost dragging the wet brush over the raised areas to allow paint to stick just to them. Make sure the ends of the horse's tail and mane are well covered to create variety in colour when the washes are applied. Paint the sides of the horse horizontally to avoid getting any paint on the recesses near the hips and other details that we want to remain the base colour.

### Step 5: Flesh wash
*Colours:* Flesh wash and Brown wash

First give the body of the horse an all-over wash using Vallejo Flesh wash. This will help to give a chestnut look to the horse. Once this had dried,

give the deeper areas of shadow, such as by the horse's hips, and other deep muscle recesses, a wash using Brown wash. Apply this only to those areas using a size 2 brush. Any messy areas can be easily wiped away using your finger.

This wash will help to give further shadows to the muscles without making the entire horse very dark, and changing the nice chestnut colour that has been created.

### Step 6: Tail and mane wash
*Colours:* Burnt Umber wash

In order to make the horse's tail and mane stand out from its body colour, use a different wash from the washes that were used on its body. To achieve this, apply Burnt Umber wash over the tail and mane

STEP 5: Applying the Flesh wash.

STEP 6: The mane and tail washes.

generously, but taking care not to get this on the horse's body.

The horse could easily be washed all over with the same colour as in the previous step if time was an issue in painting large numbers of horses.

### Step 7: Socks and hooves
*Colours:* Bone White, White, London Grey and Medium Grey

The first decision to make at this stage is which of the horse's feet best suit socks, if any. This can be affected by the previous stages as to how brown or grey the legs are. The base colour for the socks is Bone White. Paint this neatly around the hooves and in a more jagged line on the legs. Also paint a small stripe of Bone White on the horse's nose at this stage. Make the highlight for these areas using white, and apply it using vertical stripes to enhance the jagged line of the socks.

Paint the hooves using a mix of London Grey and Medium Grey. It doesn't matter if these colours aren't mixed properly as horses' hooves can have this varied mix of colours.

### Step 8: The eyes and other details
*Colours:* Brown Rose, Flat Brown, White, Black and Dark Grey.

The figure is now almost finished, and all that remains to paint are the last few details. First of all paint the eyes and the nostrils black, and the recess between the lips. Then mix together some Flat Brown and Black, and apply this colour to the eyes.

STEP 7: Painting the socks and hooves.

STEP 8: Completing the eyes and final details.

Then place a tiny dot of white at the back of each eye using a very fine brush. This finishes the eyes.

The final detail to add is the horse's nose. Dry brush this lightly using Dark Grey, trying to avoid getting any of the grey paint in the horse's nostrils. Then apply a small amount of Brown Rose to the front of the horse's top lip and nose. The horse I used for reference had a grey spot in the pinkish area of its nose, so I added this with a tiny dot of Dark Grey. Once this was painted the horse was complete!

## PAINTING A GREY HORSE USING LAYER PAINTING

This last step-by-step guide demonstrates how to layer paint horses, and is another way of painting horses from the previous two methods. This method is more time consuming, but is ideal for generals and personality figures that you want to stand out from the rest of your army. The horse described is a grey, and the guide shows how to add dapples to the coat colour, often seen on a grey horse.

### Step 1: Undercoating
*Colours:* Black spray paint

As with all the previous miniatures, the process of painting this horse begins with undercoating. When spraying the model make sure the spray reaches under the belly of the horse and around the inside of the legs. The undercoat on this particular figure will mainly act as something for the following layers of paint to adhere to. I prefer to use spray as it is fast, and it also gives a very even coating when applied using several thin coats. The even coating is especially important when using the layering technique, as any uneven areas will really show using this method.

### Step 2: Base shade
*Colours:* London Grey

Apply London Grey all over the body of the horse, making sure the areas under the legs are also covered. The base shade for this horse is easy enough to apply, though it does need a good even coat of paint to work well. It is important that none of the black undercoat shows through, as London Grey is the colour that we want to show through where needed. It doesn't matter if a little grey paint goes on the horse's mane or its tail as this can be tidied up with black paint later on in the process.

### Step 3: Mid-Tones
*Colours:* London Grey and Light Grey

Apply two mid-tone layers to this horse, both a mix of London Grey and Light Grey. The first layer is roughly equal amounts of both colours. The second layer is about three parts Light Grey and one part London Grey. Paint the colours over the muscle

STEP 1: Undercoating using black spray primer.

STEP 2: Painting the base shade using London Grey.

STEP 3: The mid-tones.

areas of the horse. Paint the colour more or less solidly across the back of the horse, but apply it in streaks down its flanks.

Apply the second mid-tone more delicately than the first but in the same areas, allowing the previous shade still to be seen.

### Step 4: Leg shading
*Colours:* Dark Grey, Black and Light Grey

Grey horses often have darker knee joints, so for the first layer of shading use some Dark Grey. Flick the paint very roughly up and down over these areas to cover them just enough. The second layer is an equal mix of Black and Dark Grey. Apply this in exactly the same way, only make sure that the area covered is smaller. This allows the first shading layer still to be seen at the top and bottom of all the knee joints.

To tidy up the lower leg mix some Light Grey with some of the remaining Dark Grey and flick it over the horse's fetlocks and pasterns (its ankles). This returns those areas to about the same colour as the upper body.

STEP 4: Leg shading.

## Step 5: Highlights

*Colours:* Light Grey and Pale Grey Blue

Three highlight layers are added to the horse at this stage. The first is Light Grey on its own, the second is an equal mix of Light Grey and Pale Grey Blue, and the third is just Pale Grey Blue on its own. Add water to the paint on all the layers; this makes the paint easier to work with, and slightly transparent as well. Concentrate the layers on the muscle areas, and apply the paint in a streaky style. Also add highlights to the horse's fetlocks and pasterns (its ankles) and its face at this stage. When highlighting around the knee joints take care to flick the paint lightly across the darkened areas, which helps to blend these two different areas of colour.

## Step 6: The mane and tail

*Colours:* Medium Grey, Ivory and White

The base shade for both the mane and the tail is Medium Grey from Vallejo. This colour has a creamy brown tinge to it, which makes it ideal for the mane and tail of this horse. Take care when painting around the mane on the horse's face and near its ears to avoid getting any of the new colour on its flesh. Once this has dried, then the tail can be highlighted.

STEP 5: Adding the highlights.

STEP 6: The first highlight stage of the mane and tail.

STEP 6: The second highlight stage of the mane and tail.

Drag the three highlight layers across the raised areas so that the newer paint only stays on the raised areas, allowing the base shade still to be seen. The first highlight is a mix of Medium Grey and Ivory, the second is just Ivory, and the third is just White. Start these highlight layers further down the mane and the tail each time you apply them to create a vignette in the colours used.

### Step 7: Dappling
*Colours:* Pale Grey Blue and Ivory

There are two layers of dappling applied to the middle area of the horse. These only go slightly into the dark grey on the legs, and only partially up the horse's neck. The first layer is a mix of Pale Grey Blue and Ivory. Apply this with a size 2 brush, and add water to make the paint a little more translucent. Dab this on using the point of the brush. Then apply a second layer using just a watery Ivory paint. Paint this in the same way, but add an uneven and less generous number of spots. Place the Ivory ones mainly over the more prominent raised areas such as the hips and the main muscles of the horse.

None of this is hard to do, but it does liven up a plain grey horse and make it more interesting. The most important part of this process is adding a little water to the paint to make it more translucent and less garish.

STEP 7: Applying the dappling.

## Step 8: The final details

*Colours:* White, Flat Brown, Black Grey, Black, Ivory and Pale Grey Blue

There are quite a few little extra details to add to this horse to complete it. First of all add extra streaks to the horse's fetlocks and pasterns (its ankles) using Ivory paint. Then paint the eyes with Black before painting a circle of Flat Brown on them. Apply a tiny dot to the back of each eye using Ivory paint. The eyes are now finished.

Use Black Grey to paint the hooves as a base shade, then a mix of Pale Grey Blue and Black Grey to add a layer of paler streaks to the hooves.

Next paint some watery Black Grey over the horse's nose. Use black paint to fill in the horse's nostrils, and to paint a line between its lips. Finally use a mix of White and Pale Grey Blue to add an extra layer of lightness to the horse's face, especially around the top of its nose and eyes.

These little additions are almost imperceptible at first, but on closer inspection you will see they are the details that bring the horse to life!

STEP 8: Applying the final details to complete the model.

# EXAMPLES OF PAINTED HORSES

## Confederate General

This general rides a simply painted bay horse with a black mane and tail, which have been dry brushed with a dark grey. The body has been painted with a mixture of layering and then washes to bring out the muscle definition. The general has been painted using the combination technique. Once painted, the horse was then based on a plastic base, stones were added to the filler, and when this was dry, the base was painted. When the paint was dry, a burnt umber wash was then applied. Finally static grass tufts and a yellow flower tuft were added to complete the model.

A Confederate General.

*PAINTED BY STEVE BARBER.*

## Union General

This officer rides a darker bay horse than his Confederate counterpart. Its mane and tail are very dark and have been dry brushed and washed, as described for the model of the Confederate general. The addition of white socks on two of its legs and a dash of white on its nose give lighter detail to this miniature. The Union general has been painted using the combination technique. The miniature was then based on a round plastic base in the same way as its Confederate counterpart, with a few select stones and some yellow flowers.

A Union General.

*PAINTED BY STEVE BARBER.*

## INTRODUCTION

Cannons and limbers and all the various types of artillery equipment require a different approach to painting. The layer style is too fussy and neat for a rugged piece of equipment such as a cannon, and equipment pieces are better suited to being painted using the dry-brushing method, or washes. Both of these methods pick out the details on the equipment very well and don't take too long to achieve decent results. Indeed, these two styles can even be mixed, as we demonstrated earlier in Chapter 4, Combination Painting.

The methods shown in this chapter will help you achieve a professional result when painting your own artillery models. They achieve a more 'rough and ready' result, which does suit the textures and grain that are to be found on artillery miniatures. Other equipment, such as limbers and field forges, can be painted using the same colours and techniques.

Military equipment such as this would be out in all weathers and caked in mud from the roads when on campaign. The gunners would obviously do their best to clean their pieces but this is harder to do whilst on campaign. So we are not trying to achieve a show-room finish with these figures. Besides using painting methods that will achieve a more 'rough and ready' finish, there are other effects and details that can be added. At the basing stage, mud can be added with filler and then painted, or earth-coloured paint can be dry brushed over the parts of the model that are most likely to become dirty. Lumps of filler can be added to the wheels and clumps of static grass then glued to them to represent sods of earth. All these little details help to give character to the finished model, and it is this attention to detail that will help your figures stand out.

## ASSEMBLING THE CANNON

It is preferable to assemble the cannon before painting it, and all the parts of the model need to be cleaned up properly before painting can begin. This can be done with a scalpel and, if required, a file. Once all the pieces have been cleaned and are free of vent sprues and flash, the model can then be painted.

The next stage of the assembly process is to glue the parts of the model together, using strong superglue such as Loctite Precision. Don't use too much glue, or it will spill out of the holes in the wheels and get on your hands when you are holding the miniature waiting for it to dry. There is a tiny elevation wheel that goes on the screw under the barrel. Glue this on first and allow it to set before fixing the barrel in place. Or if you prefer, paint the barrel separately and add it after.

### HANDY HINT: KEEP OLD BRUSHES

Most old paintbrushes can be used for something, and there are painting jobs that you wouldn't want to use your best brushes for, such as tackling larger areas on buildings, all dry-brushing work, and painting bases. Even smaller brushes that no longer have a good point or any hairs left on them can still be used. Simply cut off the remaining hairs and push a pin into the end of the handle, then cut off the top of the pin using wire cutters, and file the end to a point. This will make a great modelling tool for conversion work.

The last part of the assembly is the chain, which is added after the cannon is painted and varnished. This is a nice detail, but it is an optional extra. Most artillery models won't come with a length of fine chain, so it depends which company you source your miniatures from. The chain is quite fiddly to add, and is best done by putting a tiny dab of superglue on one of the hooks where the chain should hang. Then dangle the chain end on to this glue and let it dry for a few seconds. Then dab some more glue on to the other hook, and use a pin to attach the chain to the glue on this hook. The end of the pin will go into the chain link so you can direct it on to the glue quite easily. The model is then ready for basing.

## PAINTING A CONFEDERATE CANNON USING DRY BRUSHING

### Step 1: Undercoating
*Colours:* Black spray paint

The first stage of the process is to undercoat the miniature, and it is important because it will help the later layers of paint adhere to the metal model. The chosen colour of undercoat also helps to influence the overall finished effect of the miniature: it is essentially your canvas. For artillery and equipment a black undercoat is preferable, as any small area you miss will just look like a dark shadow. Car spray paint in a matt black is good for this as it covers well in a smooth layer and is cost effective. Spraying is also a fast way of undercoating a large number of figures at once.

Always use spray paint outside due to the fumes. Also when spraying, group the models close together on newspaper so as not to waste paint. Spray one side at a time, leaving a good ten minutes before turning them over to paint the other side. It may take a couple of coats on each side to give a good, even covering. Try not to use too much paint at once as painting in thin layers gives the best result.

### Step 2: Painting the base shades
*Colours:* Extra Dark Green and Gold Brown

Most Civil War artillery pieces were painted an Olive Drab colour. It is possible to purchase a colour like this, but for this project I have mixed the colour from those supplied in the Vallejo American Civil War set.

Mix a small amount of Gold Brown with some Extra Dark Green to create the base shade for the cannon. The Extra Dark Green colour isn't a bright green anyway, but the small amount of Gold Brown helps to muddy and lighten the colour enough to create a good base shade for artillery. Apply this with a bigger brush, being sure to paint all the hard-to-get-at woodwork areas. It doesn't matter if paint ends up on other areas at this stage. Dry brushing is not the neatest method, and all of this can easily be tidied up later on.

### Step 3: Mid-tone dry brush
*Colours:* Extra Dark Green and Gold Brown

Use the same colour that was mixed up for the base shade, but add some more Gold Brown to this mix: this helps to lighten it enough to create a

STEP 1: Undercoating with black spray primer.

STEP 2: Adding the base shades.

STEP 3: Dry brushing the mid-tones.

STEP 4: Adding the highlights.

good mid-tone colour. Coat the brush in the paint, then wipe off most of the paint on a tissue before brushing the brush across the model. A reasonable amount of pressure has to be used with the brush strokes to achieve the desired effect.

Don't worry about neatness at this stage, but make sure that most of the paint is wiped off the brush before using it. If it isn't, it will leave noticeable smears across the model as opposed to highlighting the grain. This can really spoil the look of the finished piece. So when dry brushing it is often necessary to reapply paint and wipe it off quite a few times to achieve the best result possible.

### Step 4: Highlight dry brush
*Colours:* Extra Dark Green, Gold Brown and Bone White

Once again, the previously mixed colour forms the base for the next shade. This time add Bone White to the colour on the mixing tile – and you will need to add quite a lot of Bone White to make a pale, almost pastel green. This colour will be the final highlight on the model. Using the method described in the previous step, brush the highlight colour across the model.

Make sure that most of the paint is wiped off the brush before use, and when dry brushing never mix water with the paint as this will make the paint smear. You need to apply a reasonable amount of pressure to the brush when dry brushing to achieve good contact. This final highlight should really bring out

the raised edges on the miniature and give it some life, even if it may look messy as well.

### Step 5: Blacking
*Colours:* Black

The next stage of the process is to paint over any messy areas – and as you can see, dry brushing will certainly create messy areas on the model you are painting. The main details that need to be corrected at this stage are the parts of the artillery piece that are made from metal – so paint the rims of the wheels, plus all the nuts and bolts on the model, in black. Then tidy up any messy marks on the barrel with black paint.

STEP 5: Blacking.

Once this has been done, paint all the small details and metal strapping along the cannon carriage edges in black. This does take a little while so you will need to be patient, but this stage is very important for the finished look of the cannon. The addition of black paint in this way will help create shadows for all the metal areas of the model once the dry-brush stage has been completed.

## Step 6: Metalwork dry brush

*Colours:* Oily Steel and Black

Once you have painted all the details and allowed them to dry, in order to bring them out more they need a subtle silvering. Oily Steel from the ACW set from Vallejo is ideal for this when used as a dry brush. Pour some paint on to the mixing tile and add a tiny amount of black to it. Then dip the dry-brushing brush into the paint, wiping off the excess paint on a tissue just as before. Then carefully brush over the areas that would be metal, such as the wheel rims and the bolts, and the strapping along the cannon carriage. Do this carefully to avoid it getting on the Olive Drab woodwork. The details don't need to be covered well, they just need to have some coverage with this colour.

## Step 7: Barrel base shades

*Colours:* Copper and Black

This particular cannon model is a 24pdr Howitzer. It was an impressive piece of field artillery. The barrel for it was cast from bronze, which is the colour we need to replicate here. Bronze paints are available,

but will not give light and shade to it, so I will show you how to create these effects.

For the base shade of the barrel mix a little black with some copper to create a dark brown/bronze, and apply this all over the barrel. Avoid getting the paint in the end of the barrel, as keeping this black helps to give it extra depth. It is best to take some time around areas where the barrel touches the black metalwork to avoid getting any bronze on these areas. In fact it doesn't matter if these hard-to-reach places near the black are left black, as they will just act as further shadows.

## Step 8: Barrel highlights

*Colours:* Copper, Gold, Silver, Dark Grey and Black

Bronze cannon barrels look great with several highlights on them, choosing colours that get progressively lighter. The highlights also look good painted more on the top of the barrel and in streaks horizontally across the barrel. This streaking simulates the effect that rain continually running down the sides of the barrel might make.

For the first highlight use just Copper on its own, then use a highlight of Gold, and then a few small highlights of a mix of Gold and Silver in equal parts. This number of highlights livens up the model, which its colour up until now has failed to do.

Finally mix some Dark Grey with some Black, and dry brush this round the muzzle of the gun to represent the powder burns made when the cannon is fired. These extra details don't take long to do, but add a great deal to the finished model.

STEP 6: Dry brushing the metalwork.

STEP 7: Adding the barrel base shades.

### Step 9: Details base shade
*Colours:* Medium Grey

By this stage the model cannon is almost finished and is starting to look the part – certainly all the main painting has been done. So now the final details can be added. The coil of rope along the carriage is the only detail still left to paint on this particular model. Use Medium Grey paint from Vallejo to paint the base shade of the rope. A darker base shade, such as Tan Earth, could be used but I prefer the rope to be paler to help it stand out more. The model is quite a drab, dark colour, so this is an opportunity to add some lighter details to it. Leave enough black on each side of the steel hooks at the top and bottom of the rope to act as further shadows.

### Step 10: Details highlight
*Colours:* Bone White and Ivory

The final step of this project is to paint each of the raised areas that are visible on the rope. Paint these one at a time with an equal mix of Bone White and Ivory paint from Vallejo. This allows the Medium Grey that was used as a base shade to show through, which helps to create shadows on the recesses along the rope, giving texture and definition to that area. Paint the colour on carefully using a fine brush, taking care not to get the highlight colour in the recesses.

One of the reasons for painting the rope quite pale and bright is to show you an alternative shade to paint it compared to the darker, more 'campaign' look that is created using washes, demonstrated in the next step-by-step project 'Painting a Confederate Cannon Using Washes'.

## The Finished Cannon

Once the cannon was painted it was based with its Confederate firing crew. The artillery crew miniatures for this were all painted using the wash technique. The red facings of these artillerymen add a nice bit of colour to the otherwise grey and brown Confederate army. At the basing stage the wheels could be dry brushed brown to add some mud to the wheels, or you could add a few clumps of static grass where they have picked up sods of earth.

With two different finished models to compare in this chapter you can make up your own mind which one you prefer, and which style suits you best when you come to paint your own artillery.

STEP 8: Highlighting the barrel.

STEP 9: Painting the details base shade.

STEP 10: Adding the highlight to the details.

Massed Union artillery prepares to open fire.

STEP 1: Using black spray paint as the undercoat.

STEP 2: Painting the carriage.

## PAINTING A CONFEDERATE CANNON USING WASHES

### Step 1: Undercoating

*Colours:* Matt Black spray paint

Matt Black spray paint was used to undercoat this model in exactly the same way as in Step 1 of the dry-brushing project preceding this one. The model could be sprayed in Olive Drab if you can find the right shade of spray paint, or you could paint it in Olive Drab, though you may have to apply the paint several times to avoid bare metal showing through in any missed or chipped areas.

Spray paint works very well as it gives a good even coverage of paint on the model, whilst sometimes applying undercoat with a brush can give an uneven coverage and this can lead to fine details being filled up. It is also hard to hold the cannon when painting it, which can lead to paint being smudged or wiped off, allowing the bare metal to be seen. Using spray paint also saves you time, especially when painting quite a few miniatures at once.

### Step 2: Painting the carriage

*Colours:* Extra Dark Green, Gold Brown and Bone White

When using the wash technique the colour required for the base shade is the reverse of the dry-brushing method. So the base shade for washes is almost the same as the highlight for the dry-brushing technique. Pour some Extra Dark Green on to the

mixing tile, then add some Gold Brown to it, and finally quite a lot of Bone White. The resulting colour is not quite as pastel as the dry-brushing highlight colour, but it is noticeably pale. However, this will all change considerably when the washes are applied. This will darken the green quite a bit, and also muddy the colour, as well as getting into all the recesses and details on the model.

### Step 3: Carriage details

*Colours:* Black

The next stage of the process is to paint over any areas of the cannon that were actually metal. This

STEP 3: Painting the carriage details black.

stage is the same as for the dry-brushing technique, though the areas that need to be tidied up shouldn't be quite as messy as that method. The rims of the wheels, plus all the wheel nuts and bolts, need to be painted black, and any messy marks on the barrel can be tidied up with black paint. Once this has been completed, all the small details and metal strapping along the cannon carriage can also be painted black.

This stage is very important for the finished look of the model. These black areas will often form shadows on the model between one colour and another.

## Step 4: Painting the barrel
*Colours:* Oily Steel and Black

This particular cannon model is a 10pdr Parrott rifle, and its barrel was made from both cast and wrought iron. Once made, the barrel and other metalwork on the gun were then painted black to prevent weathering on campaign. But on a model, plain black will look very dull, and will obscure the nice details on the barrel. So in order to make the barrel of this cannon more prominent, mix together one part Black with three parts Oily Steel on the mixing tile, then paint the barrel using this colour. It should look a dark silver when complete. The barrel will be washed later, which will make it even darker but at the same time will stop it from being plain black and dull.

## Step 5: Wheel details
*Colours:* Oily Steel

Dry brush the wheel rims lightly with Oily Steel. Then paint the bolts that are on the inside of the wheel rim with Oily Steel using a fine brush. Lastly, lightly paint the metalwork around the centre of the wheels in almost a dry-brushing style – almost flick the Oily Steel across these details, taking care not to get any metal paint on the green woodwork of the wheels – though as this is all going to be covered when the wash is applied it doesn't have to be perfectly neat. But if it is neat, then there will be nothing that needs covering up with extra washing or tidying. The wheels in particular will also be dry brushed with an earth colour later, to represent the earth that has been picked up in action.

## Step 6: Other details
*Colours:* Oily Steel and Bone White

At this stage paint all the other visible metalwork details in Oily Steel. Once again use the same lazy dry-brushing technique, lightly dragging the brush across the details. On this model there were a few places where the Oily Steel went on the green, but these were very small and will disappear when the washes are applied. Whilst using the Oily Steel add a few highlights to the barrel. As the barrel was painted previously using a mix of Oily Steel and Black you could add a few light highlights across its top. Paint these horizontally across the barrel.

STEP 4: Painting the cannon barrel.

STEP 5: Adding the wheel details.

STEP 6: Adding other details.

STEP 7: Applying a wash to the carriage.

STEP 8: Applying washes to the barrel.

The final detail to add is for the rope. Paint this using Bone White. The washes will add shadows to this when they are applied.

### Step 7: Applying a wash to the carriage

*Colours:* Black wash and Brown wash

Make up a fairly even mix of Black wash and Brown wash on the mixing tile, and then apply it liberally all over the cannon model. It is impossible to hold the model whilst doing this, so wash the inner parts of the model first, such as the underneath and insides of the wheels, whilst holding the model by the carriage. Then place the model on a board or something similar and apply the wash over the rest of it. Allow plenty of wash to go into areas such as the rope so that it creates the shading needed for that area.

It is at this point that the model really comes to life artistically. There was no real shading before, and now instantly there it is.

### Step 8: Applying washes to the barrel

*Colours:* Black wash

By the time this stage has been reached the cannon already looks finished. It is now just a question of adding a few finishing touches to add greater depth to the colours used, and to help show up the details as well as possible. Apply Black wash liberally to the cannon barrel. This will flow into some of its recesses and help to blend the Oily Steel highlighting. This wash only adds a subtle change to the model, but one that is worthwhile.

The final detail to add once all the washes have completely dried is an earth dry brush to the wheels, grass clumps that will be glued on using PVA glue, and static grass. However, this is an optional extra, and in the case of both these Confederate cannons I chose to leave it off and keep it simple.

## The Finished Cannon

Once this 10pdr Parrott Rifle cannon had been painted, it was then possible to compare the two painting processes. Both techniques give a good result, even though the results are quite different. Hopefully you will be able to see which technique you prefer to use when it comes to painting your own artillery miniatures.

# EXAMPLES OF AMERICAN CIVIL WAR ARTILLERY

## Union 12pdr Napoleon

The 12pdr Napoleon was the most widely used artillery piece during the Civil War. There were quite a few variations of cannon barrels produced by numerous foundries. This model was painted using a combination of dry brushing and washes. The barrel was painted using a number of different metallic shades, from dark copper to pale gold. The brush strokes were passed across the barrel, and made shorter as the colours became lighter. Some blackening was added around the muzzle of the cannon to show it had been used.

The model is based on a rectangle MDF base from East Riding Miniatures. During the basing process a few clumps of earth were added to the wheels, as well as some dirt, by dry brushing with a brown paint.

## Ruined Cannon

This particular model is available from Steve Barber Models and makes a rather useful marker model for wargaming. It was painted using a combination of dry brushing and washes. The barrel was painted using horizontal stripes of layers of progressively lighter metallic paints. The completed model was then based on a round MDF base from East Riding Miniatures. Unusual models such as this can make a nice change from painting the normal rank and file of the army you are working on, as well as being useful markers when wargaming. They also provide an opportunity for you to express your creativity, especially when it comes to basing.

## Union 20pdr Parrott Rifle

This was a big powerful gun, one of the most powerful used in the field during the American Civil War. This particular model was painted using

A 28mm Union 12pdr Napoleon cannon being fired.

*PAINTED BY STEVE BARBER.*

a combination of dry brushing and washes. The shade of olive green was mixed by eye, and was the standard colour for Union artillery during the war. The barrel on this cannon was black so it was easy to paint. I added the same details as the 12pdr Napoleon

during basing to give some realism and dirt. Both of these models had the small piece of chain added that comes with the Steve Barber Models kit. This is intricate to fit, but really completes the model once added and is a nice touch.

LEFT: A destroyed cannon.
*PAINTED BY STEVE BARBER.*

BELOW: A Union 20pdr Parrott rifle being loaded.
*PAINTED BY STEVE BARBER.*

# Varnishing, Basing and Finishing Miniatures 7

## THE DIFFERENT TYPES OF VARNISH

There are three types of varnish available for use with miniatures: matt, satin and gloss. These varnishes come in bottles and as sprays, and are available from a number of manufacturers. Matt varnish tends to be the type most widely used, but the other two still have their uses when finishing a miniature. When varnishing it is important to give the figure an even, light coat, whether by brush or spray. Don't put on too much, and if it is a spray varnish it should be used in a well ventilated area, or outside. Temperature can also be important to some varnishes, so read the instructions carefully before use, otherwise it may not work as intended.

### Matt Varnish

A matt finish is best suited to most types of clothing and flesh tones on a figure, and as indicated above, is the most widely used type of varnish for wargames' models. In fact many wargamers only use matt varnish, regardless of the material represented on the figures, as most of the time they are seen on the wargames table at arm's length. Matt varnish is intended to dull paints that have been used to paint the miniatures, and to remove any shine that may be present.

Quite a few of these varnishes are milky in colour. All varnishes need to be shaken well before use to blend all the compounds in the bottle. The varnish needs to be applied evenly to avoid it pooling in deep recesses on the figure.

### Satin Varnish

Satin varnish gives a finish somewhere between gloss and matt. It can give contrast to the different finishes on a miniature, and is used where a gloss finish would be too shiny. Cannon barrels that have dulled due to use in all weathers could be varnished with a satin

finish. Once again this varnish needs to be applied evenly and not too thickly to avoid it pooling in deep recesses on the figure. If this happens it can leave milky puddles on finished miniatures and ruin all the time and effort you have put into painting them.

### Gloss Varnish

Gloss varnish will give a shiny finish, and is quite often tougher than the others, offering the finished miniature more protection. It is for this reason that some figure painters will apply a coat of gloss varnish to their miniatures first, and once this is very dry, will apply a coat of spray matt over the top to dull it back down. It is ideally suited for use on metals and anything that in real life would have a shine to it. A polished cannon barrel that had not had much weathering could be finished with a gloss varnish. Unlike matt varnish, gloss varnishes usually require white spirit to clean the brush after use, as they are not water based.

### Creating Effects with Varnish

After all the hard work you have put into painting your figures it is important to use the right varnish to protect them. But besides just protecting the model, you can also use varnish to create different finishes on different areas of the same miniature. For example, on a cannon, the barrel can be painted with a gloss or satin varnish to give the metal a shinier finish from the rest of the model. These effects can bring a different dimension to an otherwise matt figure.

## BASING MINIATURES USING MDF OR PLASTIC BASES

Bases are available commercially in many materials, or you can easily make your own. I generally use

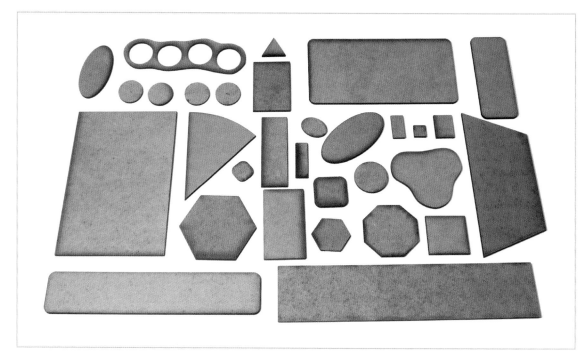

Just some of the many shapes and sizes of MDF bases that are available from East Riding Miniatures.

MDF bases from East Riding Miniatures. They have an extensive range of shapes and sizes that will undoubtedly cover most requirements, and their mail order service is excellent. They will also cut them to size if you need for base sizes that aren't listed on their website. This can be most useful for fences or other scenery that might require an odd shape or size of base. All the fences featured in this book were based using specially cut bases, which East Riding Miniatures made for me.

Plastic bases are also a good option and widely available from a number of companies. They are strong and sturdy like the MDF bases, but they do tend to raise the miniature up higher than most MDF bases. This isn't to everyone's taste, and you tend to find these more commonly used on fantasy miniatures or miniatures used in skirmish or role-playing games. These are normally available in square, round and rectangle shapes and come in a number of different sizes.

Both types of base can be treated in the same way as far as basing techniques are concerned. The basing material will stick to them in the same way, though it may take a little longer to dry on plastic bases, as these are less absorbent. Once the filler

is dry, both types of base can be painted using the same method of basing. Base sizes are normally suggested by a particular set of wargaming rules, and are generally based on a ground scale and figure scale that the rules require to work properly.

Aesthetically the most important factor to consider is using the right size base for the miniature or miniatures you are basing. Too small, and the figures will be cramped and there will be no room for scenic details. Too large, and they will be more awkward to move and will take up more table space. A base that is too large can also make it difficult to play a game due to the miniatures not being able to get close enough to each other to be in contact.

## Building up a Base using Filler, Rocks and Stones

There are quite a few commercially available basing textures you can purchase, but I have always used tiling grout on the bases for my figures. It is easily available, works well and is cost effective. Before you start applying the filler on your bases it's a good idea to have a few pots of different types and sizes of stones to hand. I have a coarse type of sand for the smallest stones, as well as a couple of sizes of stones that are available from Steve Barber Models.

If possible it is a good idea to have a separate area to use as a basing station. Basing can be messy, and you don't want sand or static grass getting on your painting area and on to your figures. Use a dinner tray or something similar to catch spilt sand or stones during basing. This material can then be reused when needed. This will also stop the spilt material from spreading around the room. Static grass in particular can get everywhere, and it's a good idea to try and contain it if possible.

The filler can be applied using a coffee stirrer or flat tool of some kind. It is best dabbed on to the base in a few areas and then spread around the bases of the figures as neatly as possible. If the filler is quite thick then it can be thinned with a drop or two of water on the tool you are using. The filler can be bevelled around the edge of the base by sloping the tool downwards towards the edge of the base. Spread thinly, this type of filler usually dries in approximately an hour.

Once the filler has been added, sprinkle the coarse sand over the base first and shake off the excess sand. Then drop on a few smaller stones and one or two larger ones. It's important not to overdo the number of stones you use. When basing a regiment of miniatures, some bases are best left without the larger stones, and others should just have a choice stone added in the right place. This variation can really enhance the finished models.

## Applying Static Grass and Tufts

For years I have applied static grass by using a layer of PVA glue and then sprinkling it on. Then I hold the miniature upside down, tap the bottom of the base and blow away the excess grass. This is the simplest and easiest method of applying static grass, and has always given me a result I was happy with. But recently I have discovered a product called Flockbox, which is available online from Warpainter. Quite simply it uses a small current of electricity to make the grass stand on its end, thereby achieving a more realistic effect.

If you want to use commercially available scenic items then there are some brilliant products available. Tajima1 makes a fabulous range of easy-to-use and

An example of a Tajima1 box of grass tufts.

Three examples of boxes of grass tufts that are available from WarWorld Scenics.

very detailed grass tufts and scenic elements and flowers. These come on shiny paper and peel off ready to apply thanks to the tacky glue they are made with. Their scenic elements are thoughtfully made details, combining several grass and flower or moorland tufts together on one item. Sometimes these need trimming with scissors to fit on bases that have several miniatures on them, but they really enhance the miniatures they are based with, which is the aim of any modeller.

War-World Scenics also produces a large and excellent range of static grass, as well as static grass tufts and other ready-to-use basing products. They are available in a variety of colours and lengths, and also tend to be slightly different shades of greens and browns from those used by Tajima1. Some of the War-World Scenics static grass was used to make grass tufts with the Flockbox during the tutorial in this chapter, and I was very happy with the results it achieved.

## THE FLOCKBOX

Flockbox is a brilliant gadget available from Warpainter; you can also find it on eBay. It is a black plastic box 7 × 5in (18 × 13cm) in size with a steel plate attached to it. Quite simply it uses a small current of electricity to make the grass stand on its end, thereby achieving a more realistic effect than just sprinkling the grass on the base. The Flockbox

comes with a DVD that has plenty of examples and a great tutorial on how to make your own grass tufts and how to base figures, as well as all the wires, battery pack and clasps that you will need. It also comes with a number of silicone paper sheets for you to test out your own tuft-making skills.

There are some other essential things you will need to purchase before you can make your own grass tufts, such as:

- A small steel plate
- Some small craft pegs
- A kitchen sieve
- Carpet tackifier
- Static grass

A number of companies now produce static grass and flock, which are available in a number of types, sizes and colours to choose from. So it takes a bit of looking to find the right ones for your project. The static grass from War-World Scenics is excellent, and I have used theirs to produce a number of different grass tufts seen on the miniatures featured in this book. You can use normal PVA glue to make grass tufts, but it doesn't give quite as good a result as carpet tackifier. The difference between them is that carpet tackifier remains tacky for a long time, making it ideal for grass tufts that you can simply peel off when you need to use them. Once you have assembled all the materials you need you can try making your own grass tufts.

RIGHT: The Flockbox, available from Warpainter.

BELOW: All the equipment required to use the Flockbox.

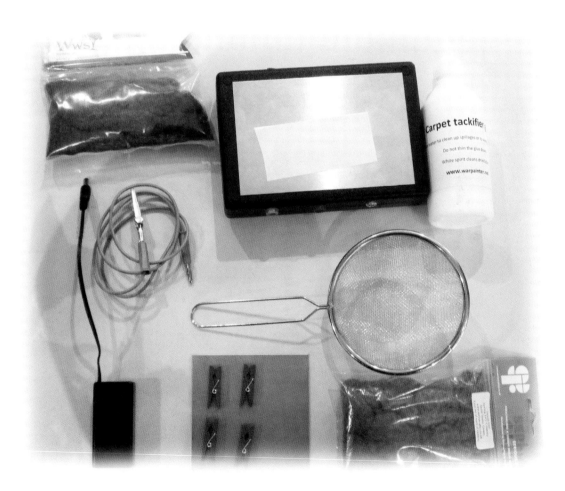

A Union Brigade attacks the
Confederate position on the ridge.

# MAKING GRASS TUFTS IN FOUR STEPS

### Step 1: Setting up

Insert a battery into the battery pack of the Flockbox, and insert the green wire into the green hole in the Flockbox. Attach the clip to the other end of the green wire, and it should be ready to use. Before you start, set everything up that you will need. Place some static grass into the sieve and place this on an old plate. Then attach a sheet of silicone paper to the steel sheet with a craft peg at either end. These pegs will hold the paper in place during the flocking process. Then place blobs of carpet tackifier of your chosen shape or size on to the silicone paper. Then everything is set up.

Note that the guidelines advise never to have your mobile phone on you whilst using the Flockbox, so it is just as well to follow this precaution.

### Step 2: Sieving

First make sure the Flockbox and its battery pack are switched off. Then place the sieve over the base plate of the Flockbox and rub the static grass around the inside of the sieve until it there is a good layer covering the base plate. This loosens the static grass and prevents lumps attaching themselves to the glue. Making grass tufts is messy, and it may be worthwhile placing the Flockbox on a dinner tray or similar to catch most of the stray grass. Of course the left-over grass can be reused time and time again,

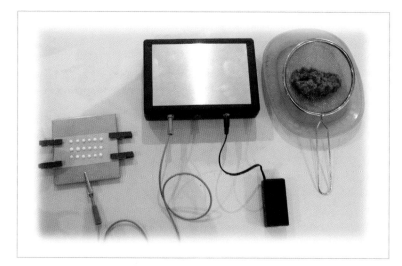

The Flockbox once it is set up and ready to go.

Sieving static grass on to the Flockbox metal plate.

so it's worth trying to retain as much of it as possible. At this stage you could mix flocks together to create mixed lengths or mixed coloured tufts.

### Step 3: Get flocking!
Once everything is ready to go it is time to get flocking! Turn on the battery pack first, then pick up the base plate by the pegs so that the blobs of glue face downwards. Then switch to holding the plastic part of the green clip. It can give you an electric shock, so be sure to follow closely all the instructions that come with the Flockbox. Only hold the plastic or the wood, never the metal. Whilst holding the green plastic clip, switch on the Flockbox. You will instantly notice activity on the Flockbox as the current

charges the grass. Then pass the steel plate and glue blobs over the static grass. Make sure it is a few inches from the static grass as it passes over. The grass is quickly attracted to the glue and the tufts are soon finished. During this process the remaining grass dissipates a few feet from the box.

### Step 4: Finishing
The result is very pleasing. The finished grass tufts were quick and easy to make and look very professional. Like this, making grass tufts is so much fun! Once they are finished they need to be unclipped carefully from the steel base plate and left for twenty-four hours to let the glue dry properly.

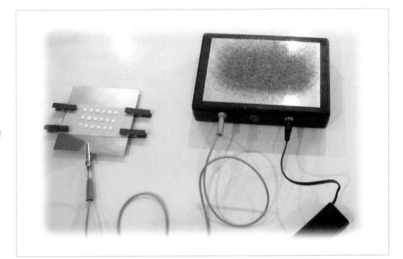

Ready to flock!

The charged static grass going up on to the metal plate.

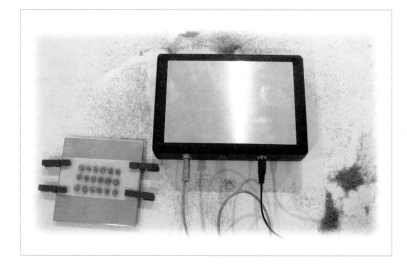

The tufts are made.

The finished grass tufts.

My grass tufts. One row has had PVA glue brushed across them, and then they were pushed into yellow scatter to create flower tufts.

They mustn't be touched at all during this drying time, as it will ruin the tufts.

Once the tufts are dry, they can be turned into flower tufts by just brushing PVA glue lightly over the tops of the tufts and sprinkling on a coarser type of coloured flock. All in all, the Flockbox is a great idea, and in a very short time and with little effort you will be able to create fabulous bases for your miniatures and terrain.

## FINISHING A MINIATURE

Finishing a miniature is a stage of painting a figure that is often overlooked, but it is important to show off all your hard work in the best way possible. It's a good idea to think about basing the miniature before you actually do it. That way you can plan the effect you want to create, and make sure you have all the necessary scenic items required to achieve that effect.

## PAINTED OR PRINTED FLAGS

Depending on the complexity of the flag in question it may be possible to paint it. The flags used during the American Civil War varied hugely in their design and the level of details used. The regimental colours used by the Union were often incredibly elaborate and would take a long time to paint by hand. Such elaborate flags are therefore not worth painting for wargames' armies, especially when high quality printed flags are available to purchase. But it is often possible to paint some Confederate or Corps flags. Most of the time I use printed flags for my figures, which are very high quality and achieve a good result very easily.

Wargamers and modellers are now incredibly lucky to have companies that produce high quality printed miniature flags. The American Civil War is particularly well covered, with flags for both sides readily available. The flags used in this book are produced by GMB designs, Flags of War and Battleflag. All three companies produce fantastic, high quality, printed paper flags, and have considerable ranges for the American Civil War and other periods of history. The paper that all three companies use is quite thick and very good quality, so it is quite durable and won't tear too easily. The print quality is excellent for all three companies. Every detail of the flags is lovingly reproduced for the wargamer to savour.

The brilliant New York legion's flags available from Battleflag.

Examples of some of the many excellent Confederate flags that are available from Flags of War.

The Battleflag flags are sold on A4 sheets, and these sheets are themed. So one sheet might contain all the flags of a particular brigade, such as Hood's Texas Brigade. They also produce an excellent sheet on New York's Foreign Legions, which has some unusual flags to add to your Union army. These New York regiments were made up from immigrants from Italy, Ireland and France, and comprised some of the most notable regiments of the Civil War. Indeed, the Irish regiments were some of the finest in the Union Army. Each flag sheet often has a photo of the general who commanded the particular brigade, which is a nice touch.

The Flags of War flags are aimed at each regiment and will often have the state flag and the regiment flag on one sheet of quality paper. The company makes a good and growing range of flags for the American Civil War in 28mm, with the Confederate army being particularly well catered for. They also produce a good range of Corps flags, as well as American Civil War flags in 40mm scale. Their contact details are listed at the back of this book,

along with a list of useful companies for wargaming in general.

The flags need to be cut out with either a scalpel or scissors, whichever you find easier. I usually use a scalpel as I find I can control the blade more easily around the fringed edges that the flags sometimes have. Once the flag has been cut out, apply a thin coat of craft glue, making sure the underside of the flag is completely covered. It is especially important to get the glue to the corners of the flag so these don't become unstuck once the flag is on the miniature. Try to avoid getting glue on the colour flag surface underneath.

When the paper is covered in glue, the flag can be folded around the painted flagpole. When doing this, leave a little spare space on the pole at the top where the finial will be placed. Once dry, the flagpole can then have any painted finials glued to its top. Then it can be glued on to the miniature with superglue.

Opposite are some of the gorgeous examples of the flags available from Flags of War and from Battleflag.

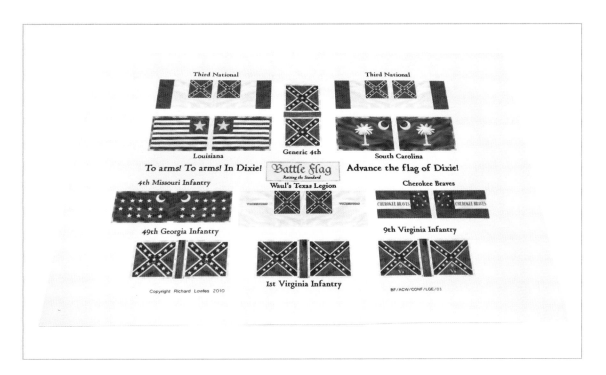

One of the Confederate flag sheets available from Battleflag.

Examples of some of the many excellent Union flags that are available from Flags of War.

# BASING MINIATURES IN EIGHT STEPS

## Step 1: Gluing the miniature to the base

*You will need:* An MDF base and superglue

Glue the figure on to an MDF base from East Riding Miniatures, using Loctite superglue. I usually put a blob of superglue on the base and then place the figure on top of it. Only a small amount is required, approximately half the size of the base of the actual miniature. Then allow the glue to dry. Even with superglue it is best to allow the glue to dry overnight, or for at least five hours. The worst thing is for the model to come off when you are putting the filler on. In this instance you would need to clean the base, or use a new base that wasn't wet, so the cleaned base of the miniature sticks to the MDF base.

## Step 2: Applying filler to the base

*You will need:* Filler such as tiling grout

Next apply filler to the base using a thin wooden spatula. Work this round the base, taking care round the feet of the miniature. Rather than just putting the filler up to the base of the figure, it is often a good idea to put some on top of the base of the actual model. This way you can avoid the regular shape of the base of the miniature still being visible once the process is finished. In order to get between the feet of the figure neatly, you may need to use a modelling tool to move the filler around this area. The tool can

STEP 1: Gluing the miniature to the base.

STEP 2: Applying filler to the base.

easily be washed afterwards. Sometimes it may be necessary to dip the spatula into some water to help spread the filler around more easily.

### Step 3: Adding texture
*You will need:* Modelling sand and stones

While the filler is still wet apply coarse sand and stones. Sprinkle the sand on first and shake off the excess afterwards. It's important to get a good covering, but you don't want it to be too even. Some irregular patches will make it look better. Then begin placing the stones on the base, pushing down on them gently to secure them to the base. Once this is complete, just turn the miniature upside down and gently tap the bottom of the base. Anything that is

not quite fixed will come off, and it's better that this happens at this stage than later on.

Allow the model to dry for at least four hours otherwise the stones may come off once you start painting.

### Step 4: Painting the base colour
*You will need:* Leather Brown (from Vallejo)

Once the filler is thoroughly dry, you can apply the base coat of paint. Leather Brown from Vallejo makes a superb earth colour, though you may find other browns that you prefer, depending on the desired finish. Once again take care around the feet of the model when painting the first colour. When painting the base, be sure to apply sufficient

STEP 3: Adding some texture to the figure's base.

STEP 4: Painting the base colour using Leather Brown.

paint to avoid gaps appearing near stones. This can sometimes happen when air bubbles get trapped under the paint.

## Step 5: Shading the base
*You will need:* Tan Earth (from Vallejo)

Put some Tan Earth on the mixing tile, and take up a little on an old size 2 brush or similar. Then wipe off most of the paint on a tissue, and lightly brush over the stones on the figure's base. This should highlight the top of the stones, leaving the rest of the surface still showing the Leather Brown used earlier. Dry brushing ruins paintbrushes, and there is no way round that, so you will need to have some brushes that you can use just for this purpose.

## Step 6: Dry-brushing the base
*You will need:* Bone White (from Vallejo)

Using the same method as described previously, dry brush the Bone White over the stones. The amount of pressure you use requires some practice, as does the amount of paint to leave on the brush. To start with it is better to have too little paint on the brush than too much, as it's easier to reapply some more than to have to repaint the base.

This final highlight colour can be used to accentuate areas of the base that you want to leave uncovered, or to make some stones lighter than others. By this stage the figure's base is starting to look more complete.

STEP 5: Shading the base.

STEP 6: Dry brushing the base using Bone White.

### Step 7: Adding a wash to the base

*You will need:* Umber Wash (by Vallejo)

It isn't essential to do this step, but adding a dark brown wash over the base helps to bring out the details and gives it extra definition. To apply the wash, use a bigger brush such as a size 3, and dab the wash all over the base. It should look irregular at this stage, with some lighter and darker patches. Don't apply excessive amounts, but just enough to cover everything well. Once again, take care not to get any spotting around the miniature's feet and legs.

### Step 8: Finishing touches

*You will need:* A selection of basing materials

This is the most enjoyable part of the basing process, and perhaps the most distinctive. Choosing the different elements, such as grass tufts, branches, plants and so on, can be fun. These pieces add the finishing touches to the miniature. However, it's important not to overdo the elements on one base so as to keep the miniature looking as if it is in a natural setting. Try to choose pieces that complement each other in the way you might find in real life. Also when basing a regiment it's important not to make every base full of elements. You want to have some plain ones, and some with flowers and plants, so the figures are still the main focal point and not the amount of floral decoration that is used.

The images on p.98 illustrate two good examples of basing.

STEP 7: Applying an Umber wash to the figure's base.

STEP 8: Finishing the figure's base.

Zouaves head towards the front.

This Union battery commander has had a scenic fern and a stone-washed pebble added to his base. Flag by GMB design.
*PAINTED BY STEVE BARBER.*

These miniatures of the famous Berdan's Sharpshooters have been based effectively using some twigs for broken trees. Paper ivy was then delicately applied to the damaged tree.
*MINIATURES PAINTED BY STEVE BARBER.*

## WHY CONVERT FIGURES?

Sculptors of miniatures will definitely know the value of converting a figure to create a variant quickly and easily: it's much easier than sculpting a whole new model every time, particularly when producing a range of miniatures, as the differences between some troop types is often only very slight. It may be that only the head is different, or just some extra lace detailing work. But whatever it may be, just adding these details to a metal model with putty such as 'Green Stuff' means that completing a range of miniatures becomes more realistic than having to sculpt every single figure individually.

Not only does converting a figure save time, it also keeps continuity within a range – hats remain the same size, as do weapons and other equipment – and herein lies the value of conversions.

For a modeller, converting miniatures can be enjoyable and addictive. Once you have learned a few simple techniques you will be able to make your own unique conversions, creating unusual models that are not commercially available, and giving character to a skirmish line that would otherwise come from a packet. Converting your own miniatures, even just simple conversions, will also give you a sense of achievement. Just knowing that you were involved in how the model looks as well as how it was painted is rewarding. In fact you will probably never look at a packet of figures in the same way again – you will see the miniatures in the packet but will also be thinking of what they can be converted into!

Confederate snipers look down on the Union positions.
*PAINTED BY STEVE BARBER.*

An example of the type of conversion that can be made very simply using pieces available from Steve Barber Models.

## ESSENTIAL TOOLS FOR CONVERTING FIGURES

The following tools are needed to make conversions:

- Sculpting putty
- Modelling tools and scalpel
- Files and pliers
- Superglue
- A magnifying lamp
- A mini drill
- A mini hacksaw

### Sculpting Putty

There are many types of sculpting putty in a range of strengths and colours, with varying drying times.

You will be able to decide which ones suit you best after trying them out for yourself, but there are two that I have used for years now: Green Stuff and Milliput. They are very different from each other, but they cover the wide range of tasks asked of them, including small and large scale pieces, humans, animals and buildings – an array of objects that require quite different sculpting putty.

### Green Stuff

The most widely used putty for conversion work is 'Green Stuff' by Sylmasta. This is a two-part putty that hardens in about an hour once both of the parts are mixed together. There is a yellow side and a blue side, and once mixed they become green, hence the name 'Green Stuff'. The putty is usually supplied in a ribbon, and in order to get equal amounts, a thin strip needs to be cut from the end of the ribbon as straight as possible.

Roll the strip repeatedly in the palm of your hand in a sausage shape and then a ball, until there are no streaks in the green. The putty must be mixed well as otherwise it will still have soft areas when most of it has dried, which is definitely undesirable. The putty doesn't stick to your hands when you are mixing it.

Once it is mixed well, then it is ready to use. It will last for about forty-five minutes before it becomes too hard to use properly, so only mix what you think you will need for the area you are converting. If you try to do too much at once the putty will have dried before you have completed all the parts you were trying to convert.

ABOVE: A pot of Green Stuff available from Sylmasta.

LEFT: The roll of Green Stuff inside the pot.

BELOW: The two parts of the AB putty, which are inside the pot.

Sylmasta operate an excellent mail order service and products are dispatched very quickly.

## Milliput

I have used superfine white Milliput for twenty years, with which it is possible to get very crisp, sharp lines. Building it up in layers is the best way to sculpt with it. It is very different from Green Stuff described above. It is sticky to handle and requires water to smooth the surface. It will stick on your hands, so after mixing you may want to wash your hands before continuing.

Once set, Milliput dries very hard and is very strong. It can then be sanded and carved. It is

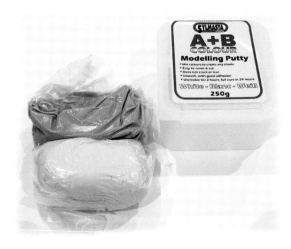

excellent for larger areas such as buildings and terrain. Most of the buildings I have sculpted were made using different packs of Milliput. The superfine white is very good for detail areas. Milliput is widely available online and in most hobby shops. The Milliput company also makes other products that are different colours and grades of coarseness.

## Modelling Tools and Scalpels

I have had the number 46 modelling tool that I use for sculpting for over twenty years, and it has certainly provided value for money.

I also have a couple of homemade pin tools that were easy to make. I removed the hairs from old paintbrushes, and snipped the heads off different sized pins. The headless pins were then forced into the paintbrush handles, using pliers to start with, and then pressing the sharp end into some wood to force it inside the handle. These are very useful, simple tools for sculpting, and are ideal for work on buttons and eyes and other fine details.

The other main tool that I use is a Swan Morten number 3 scalpel, used with their size 10a blades. It also has stood me in good stead over the years

though there have of course been countless blades over that time. Once purchased, these tools certainly are value for money.

## Files and Pliers

Files are also vital when converting miniatures, and you will need a variety of shapes and sizes in order to get into all the hard-to-reach areas of your figures. The diamond-coated ones are very good but can clog easily if used on metal, so are best reserved for filing other materials. The normal type of file is best for filing the metal that your model is made from.

Modelling pliers that are long and thin and round in shape are best for bending metal parts. This rounded shape means that the dent they make in the figure is softer and more crease like – sometimes you won't even need to fill the mark they make.

You will also require a small wire cutter. This can be useful for cutting off details, or cutting wire for drilling and pinning. Shesto make an excellent diamond file reamer and file set, which is perfect for getting into those hard-to-reach areas on a miniature. The set comes with four diamond bits and a pin vice, pen-style holder.

White Milliput.

Grey Milliput.

A diamond reamer and file set, available from Shesto.com.

## Superglue

There are many brands and types of superglue; Loctite Precision is ideal for most modelling requirements. Loctite glue has a small, pointed application nozzle, which really helps when converting or assembling miniatures for painting, as it is easy to get into small or difficult places without it spilling out on to the rest of the model. There may be stronger glues, but this one is certainly strong enough for most modelling needs. I mostly use it to glue the metal parts of miniatures together and to glue figures on to their MDF bases.

Loctite Precision also glues resin parts together well; for example it is excellent for the task of gluing together resin buildings and ships. Loctite also make superglue in a glue pen, which is useful for various modelling tasks, including gluing miniatures to their bases.

Loctite is widely available online and in many stores.

## Magnifying Lamp

Shesto make a great range of magnifying lamps that are ideal for painting and converting miniatures. The LC8093 model table magnifying lamp has a large main

The Loctite glue pen.

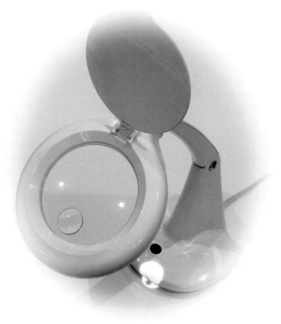

The LC8093 magnifying lamp available from Shesto.com.

lens, with a smaller, more powerful lens built into it, which is ideal for those extra fine details on faces or buttons. The LED lamp gives off a very bright white light, which shows nicely the colours you are using without changing the hue. It is lovely to use, and the magnifier is perfect for most painting needs. I would definitely recommend this magnifying lamp for painting figures.

The company also produce a larger model, and a more compact one, as well as a nice Optivisor headband for those who prefer to wear their magnifier on their head. (*See* Contact Details for Shesto's company details.)

## Mini Drills

A mini drill set for hobby work is available from Shesto. They produce quite a variety as well as supplying all of the drill bits for use with them. Most plug into the mains and have a decent length of cord to allow good movement of the drill. HSS drill bits often come separately in sets, so it is advisable to get a good selection of fine drills to go with your drill. A decent drill set should last for years and be a good investment for your hobby: my old drill set, borrowed from my Dad many years ago, is still going strong. The drill bits for mini drills do occasionally break, so be sure to have a number of spares of the main sizes you use in your drill box.

The other drill I use is the RC09X. It is part of Shesto's Rota Craft range and comes in its own bag with an assortment of tools for sanding, engraving, polishing and of course drilling. Other drill bits can be purchased separately. The drill is cordless, which is an advantage as it avoids wires potentially moving the drill bit whilst you are working.

## Mini Hacksaws

A mini hacksaw can be quite easily and cheaply obtained from Shesto.com. This simple tool is vital for miniature work, and is perfect for conversion work. It is much better suited to the small nature of converting miniatures than the larger woodworking type. Hacksaws such as this can be used for removing bases, so a figure can be pinned just by its feet to an unusual base for example, or to remove equipment from a figure that could then have Green Stuff applied over the raw metal. Whatever the use, a good hacksaw will come in very handy.

Shesto's mail order is fast and efficient. They also produce a scalpel-style saw set, where each blade in the set has a different type of saw edge to it. These are probably best reserved for light use and with plastic figures. For converting metal miniatures ideally you will need a mini hacksaw.

The RC09X drill set available from Shesto.com.

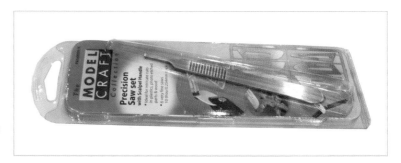

The precision saw set available from Shesto.com.

## DRILLING AND PINNING

Drilling and pinning is a useful skill when making models and converting miniatures. It can help to strengthen weak joins on a model, as well as creating armatures to sculpt on to using Green Stuff. Take care when drilling into a miniature to avoid drilling into your fingers. It is always best to hold the piece that's being drilled in an area of the model that is not right next to the drill bit, or to use a miniature vice. Miniature vices are widely available and easy to obtain.

Brass wire or florists' wire can be used to pin pieces of a model together. Once glued into a piece of the figure using Loctite superglue, they can be snipped to the right length using wire cutters. For less visible work use florists' wire: it is cheaper, and does the job perfectly well. For anything that can be seen, such as a flagpole, use brass rod. Both are available in a number of thicknesses to suit most tasks, so it's a good idea to have a selection of sizes in your modelling toolbox.

The Model Craft 14cm turntable available from Shesto.com.

## CONVERTING YOUR OWN MINIATURES

Conversions can be anything from a head swap to adding equipment. There are endless possibilities; really it is all about exploring ideas in your imagination. Look at pieces and see what may be missing from the miniatures you have, or in some cases the figures that are commercially available. Notice what other modellers have done, online or in magazines, and this can help you come up with your own ideas. Most people who convert miniatures will do so mainly to create certain special figures to add to their force. That may be a general, a vignette of a wounded soldier, a destroyed cannon: pieces like this add character to your army and create a talking point when they are viewed by other wargamers.

Some converting work involves actual sculpting using Green Stuff and is probably well beyond most novice gamers. Using Green Stuff to sculpt a face, for example, does require artistic talent and plenty of practice – but to add a patch or a rip to a pair of trousers on a miniature is certainly within the ability of most wargamers and well worth doing. Head swaps are easy to do and can add variety to a unit, or even make figures for units that are not commercially available. This is one of the best conversions you can do, and it is possible to create some great regiments for your army this way.

Also, most of the miniatures from the Steve Barber Models range (as featured in this book) are produced in three pieces, so it is easy to swap parts from one pack with another to create individual models without having to do much converting work at all! They also produce a large range of head packs, which makes conversion work even easier.

## Converting Plastic Figures

Some people prefer plastic miniatures to metal. Although they can be brittle and bayonets can sometimes break off and need to be glued back in place, the multipart nature of these figures makes them ideal for swapping parts and converting. Pieces are easy to glue in place using plastic glue, although once glued in place these pieces are well and truly stuck: this is because the plastic glue melts the two surfaces together, causing a strong bond to form.

Plastic models can of course have metal parts fixed to them as well. Indeed, many people find plastic figures too light, so they glue them on metal bases to make them heavier and therefore less likely to topple over, causing breaks to the miniatures.

When converting plastic figures you will need a good model knife to clean up the pieces and to cut pieces off the miniatures. It's also important to use the right glue. Superglue may not work too well on plastic figures, but glue for plastic models is widely available and easy to obtain. Also tools such as mini drills and Green Stuff will be useful for conversions – Green Stuff will adhere just as well to plastic models as to metal ones.

When using a mini drill on a plastic part it is important to remember not to use as much pressure when drilling. The pieces break more readily than metal, and the drill will go through the part much more quickly. Care should be taken whenever you use the mini drill. Be careful to follow the instructions that come with it, and if necessary use a small vice to hold the part that is being drilled.

# EXAMPLES OF MINIATURES MADE USING CONVERSIONS

## The Banjo Player

This figure was made from pieces from a Steve Barber Models Union artillery crew. The gunner who stands holding the sponge/rammer has two separate arms, which easily allows for these to be placed slightly differently. He is also open handed, which is ideal for posing him playing a banjo. His right forearm was bent slightly with pliers, and the dent filled with Green Stuff. The banjo was created using Milliput. Then all the pieces were glued together using Loctite Superglue. He was painted using the combination technique described in Chapter 4.

A lot of the detail was added during the basing stage. He was based on a 40mm (1.5in) round MDF basing from East Riding Miniatures. A tree stump was made by sawing in half a thicker piece of wood from a pack of scenic tree branches from Steve Barber Models. Also some of the spare bark in the pack was broken down to make suitable forest floor scatter. Another branch was cut to size and placed behind the banjo player. A small piece of paper was cut and folded to resemble a newspaper, and glued in place with PVA glue. When this was dry the newsprint was painted on with a fine brush and watery black paint.

The final detail was a coffee pot from the Tennessee Thompson miniature set. A couple of grass tufts were added to the base – and he was complete!

## The Artillery Standard Bearer

This is a simple but effective conversion. The model was created from a standing Union artilleryman available as part of a pack from Steve Barber Models. The torso of the figure was intended to hold a lanyard to fire a cannon, but his arm was bent into a different position using pliers and the dents this made in the metal were then filled with Green Stuff. When this simple conversion had been made, he was painted using the combination method. Once that had been done he was ready to hold the artillery standard. This particular flag was available from GMB designs. The flagpole was topped off using a finial painted gold, and glued on with superglue. This is much easier to do once everything else has been

This Union artilleryman playing a banjo was a pretty simple conversion, mostly from parts available from Steve Barber Models. *PAINTED BY STEVE BARBER.*

A Union battery commander. The standard bearer was a simple conversion. *FLAG BY GMB DESIGN. PAINTED BY STEVE BARBER.*

done. He was then based on a 50mm (2in) round MDF base from East Riding Miniatures, along with an artillery officer from a Union firing pack.

## The 69th NYSM

This is a miniature of the Zouave company of the 69th New York State Militia, which fought for the Union during the Civil War. Steve Barber Models produces separate head packs that are ideal for converting figures such as this. This model is created from a Union Zouave torso and musket arm, Confederate legs and a Havelock hat head. This mix-and-match ability of the miniatures they produce makes them highly suitable for simple conversions such as this.

Once the figure was glued together he needed a waist sash, so a small amount of Green Stuff was

The converted miniature of the 69th NYSM. Only a small amount of Green Stuff was required to make this simple conversion.

The finished painted version of the 69th NYSM. This was an easy and effective conversion to make.

A simple conversion created this ammunition carrier for the 54th Massachusetts.

used to create this. Once it had been mixed it was rolled into a thin sausage and then pressed on to the figure, flattened down and then trimmed. A few lines were pressed into it using a modelling tool, to create texture on the sash. A little extra Green Stuff was used to fill a small gap where the arm had been glued on. Once this had all been completed, the model was painted using the combination method. This was a nice miniature to paint, and had not taken long to convert.

## SUMMARY

This chapter just introduces the idea of converting figures, as many modellers may never have thought about trying it. A subject as varied and diverse as converting miniatures could have a whole book written about it, including step-by-step demonstrations showing different conversion ideas and methods. There are various techniques to talk about, and far too many things to discuss within the confines of this one chapter, which is why there is no more than an outline of the tools required, and just a few examples from my own collection to demonstrate what is possible with a little time and thought.

Conversions, whether in metal or plastic, can be as simple or as sophisticated as you want, and it's up to the modeller to see the possibilities in a miniature and then make them real.

I hope some of the information and ideas contained in this chapter might inspire you to try converting your own miniatures – and if they go wrong at first it doesn't really matter: just keep trying and it will work eventually. Practice makes perfect! Even if it is a simple head swap or putting a patch on the trousers of the model you are going to paint, it will still be *your* work and the figure will probably be unique to you. So why not get your thinking cap on, look at that humble miniature that has been sitting on your painting desk and that you have been meaning to paint for a while and have a go at converting a figure of your own!

# 9 Buildings and Scenery

## THE IMPORTANCE OF TERRAIN IN WARGAMING

Terrain can be readily overlooked in wargaming. The planning and research that goes into painting an army, and then finding the best rulebook to wargame it with, can mean that attention to the terrain is left until last. There is no doubt, however, that the spectacle of a miniature battle has considerably more impact if it is fought over realistic and detailed ground. Why have fabulous troops, whose every detail you have painted with painstaking care, only to use them on a battlefield that is sadly lacking in realism? But this area of wargaming has improved considerably in quality over the last twenty years or so, and today we are very fortunate in that there are numerous companies producing quality scenic items.

The following step-by-step guides show models from two companies, both of whom produce excellent miniature buildings for this period of history.

Buildings and terrain are produced in a variety of materials these days, including resin and laser-cut MDF. One of the best ranges of MDF buildings available for the wargamer is by Sarissa Precision, who make some really detailed and impressive-looking kits for the American Civil War. Their range includes the famous Dunker Church from the Battle of Antietam, as well as plantation-style houses, timber barns and bridges, and other great models that would grace your wargames' table.

Unlike most cast resin buildings, all MDF buildings must be assembled. If you prefer not to do this yourself, there are some excellent resin buildings commercially available that require little or no

The Confederate battle line. The miniatures are by Steve Barber Models.

*PAINTED BY STEVE BARBER.*

Some of the excellent MDF buildings available from Sarissa Precision.

assembly. However, for the small amount of work involved in assembling the MDF buildings, you can get some fabulous additions to your terrain.

The Sarissa Precision kits all require assembly, but this is quite easy to do. The kits come in ready-cut sheets, so all you need do is cut out the required parts and follow the assembly instructions that come with each kit. The parts must be glued together using Loctite Precision superglue. PVA glue will also work, but the pieces will take longer to bond together. Gluing is straightforward as the parts come with plugs and holes, so the pieces are easy to fit to each other. However, some of these are quite delicate once cut out, so take care when fixing them together. Once assembled the buildings are reasonably tough and durable.

The first step-by-step guide uses the Dunker Church kit by Sarissa Precision. The kit consists of three sheets of 2mm MDF, and the majority of the parts just pop away from the tiny connecting sprues that hold them on the sheets. Cut the connecting sprues holding the more delicate parts with a scalpel otherwise they might break. The MDF is thin and some parts are delicate, so you need to be careful when assembling those parts. The kit comes with good instructions, so follow these.

Glue the pieces together using superglue. You need to make sure you have the pieces in the right place before gluing them, as once they are glued they don't come off. Some parts of the kit I assembled first, and then drizzled the glue through the connecting holes. You may also notice a large barn produced by this company in the photographs in this book.

## PAINTING AN MDF MODEL BUILDING IN EIGHT STEPS

### Step 1: Preparation
This first step shows the model assembled before it was painted: like this you can see the areas filled using super-fine white Milliput. A few connecting sprues remain visible once the model is assembled: to hide these, mix up the two parts of the Milliput, then using a modelling tool and some water, press and then smooth the putty over them. You can also add a row of ridge tiles to the top of the model using Milliput. These details don't have to be done, as once painted they are barely visible, but I prefer to fill them.

## Step 2: Base shades

*Colours:* Medium Sea Grey, Light Grey and Black Grey

This step takes a while and uses quite a bit of paint. As the church model is whitewashed over its walls, white is the dominant colour of the model. You could just spray it white for quickness, but the effect is better if you use a base tone, a mid-tone

and a highlight, so begin by painting the model grey for its base tone. Pour Medium Sea Grey and Light Grey by Vallejo on to the mixing tile. You will need a considerable amount to cover the model because it is so big – the pools I poured out had to be repeated five times!

Don't mix the colours, just randomly use the brush in each one to paint the building. This way the colours gain texture through the unevenness of their application, and this helps to give the building a weathered look. The model may look dark to start with, but it will end up being much lighter after the successive layers are applied.

After completing this base coat, paint the roof using Black Grey (in this case again by Vallejo). Again, a considerable amount of paint was used to cover such a large area of roof.

## Step 3: Adding the mid-tone to the walls

*Colours:* Silver Grey

To paint the mid-tone for this building you will need a very pale grey. Silver Grey is perfect for this. To avoid the building being just brilliant gleaming white and to make it look a little lived in, pour the paint on to the mixing tile and apply it with a 2in brush in an up-and-down motion. This leaves streaks running down the surface and achieves an

STEP 1: The kit is built and the filling is finished.

STEP 2: Painting the base shades.

STEP 3: Adding the mid-tone to the walls using Silver Grey.

attractively uneven, weathered look. It also leaves areas where the Medium Sea Grey and the Light Grey mix that was used for the base tone can still be seen. It also leaves areas of shadow around the windows, which helps to give definition to the building.

With a smaller brush, use the same streaking technique on the chimney and the eaves of the roof section, though be careful not to get any on the roof tiles nearby.

### Step 4: Adding the highlight to the walls
*Colours:* White

Pour white paint on to the mixing tile. Then using the 2in paintbrush again, apply streaks all over. This leaves areas where the previous three colours still show through, giving a less one-dimensional look than just painting it white would have done. With a smaller brush, use the same streaking technique on the chimney and the eaves of the roof section. Though this is quick to do, you need to apply the paint three times in total to give sufficient coverage of white.

Once you have done this you can create a different texture to the model by dipping the brush in the paint,

then wiping most of it off and stippling the walls with the remaining paint – in other words, dab the end of the brush down on the model repeatedly. This produces a random dotted texture. Continue to apply this texturing if you want a whiter finish.

STEP 4: Adding the highlight to the walls.

STEP 4: A close-up of the walls after the highlighting stage.

STEP 5: Painting the highlights
on the roof tiles using Dark Grey.

STEP 6: Adding the shutter and door base
shades using Deep Green and Silver Grey.

## Step 5: Roof tile highlights

*Colours:* Dark Grey

In order to add more detail to the very dark grey of the roof mass, use Dark Grey, which is in fact a lighter colour, to add a highlight to the roof tiles. Highlight each tile individually, as this produces the best result. You could just dry brush the roof, but this wouldn't give the same depth. Highlight each tile randomly using different patterns. Paint them in the same direction, from right to left, and do it in a downward direction. This highlighting is to make it look as if the light is landing on the tiles from the top right.

## Step 6: Shutters and door base shades

*Colours:* Deep Green and Silver Grey

Paint all the shutters and the doorframes in Deep Green. It took two coats of paint as the paint really does get absorbed into the wood quickly. Then paint all six inner panels with Silver Grey. You may need to neaten the edges of the panels with some more Deep Green paint, if there are places where the Silver Grey has gone on to the green. It isn't easy to paint the shutters neatly when they were already glued on.

With the benefit of hindsight, it may be easier to paint them first and then glue them on to the model.

## Step 7: Shutter and door highlights

*Colours:* Deep Green, Intermediate Green and Silver Grey

Create two highlights on the shutters and doors, the first a mix of Deep Green and Intermediate

STEP 7: Painting the highlights
on the shutters and doors.

STEP 7: Close-up of the door after the highlights have been added.

BELOW LEFT:
STEP 8: Adding the finishing touches to the building.

BELOW RIGHT:
STEP 8: Close-up of the finished building.

Green, and the second the same mix but with some Silver Grey added to give a lighter green for the final highlight. Apply both from top to bottom and right to left using streaks. This continues the idea of light hitting them from the right. These effects help bring depth and texture to the building.

### Step 8: The building details

*Colours:* White, Dark Grey wash, Deep Green and Burnt Umber wash

By this stage the building is virtually finished, and it is just a case of adding a few final details. For the first stage paint the six door panels on each of the doors with White for its final highlight; again, apply

this using streaks going from right to left and in a top-to-bottom motion. Then use a series of washes to add some extra weathering.

First of all mix some Deep Green paint with some Burnt Umber wash, and thin it with some water.

A Union Brigade advances past a farm.

Apply this under all the windows and shutters, on the chimney and around the doorframe, and the eaves on the roof section. Apply the wash as though it were running down the walls and mostly on the edge of the shutters, where the water would run the most. Then apply a watery Burnt Umber wash on the tops of the windows and under the eaves on the side of the building. Finally apply a Dark Grey wash to the edges of the steps, and then another with a little Deep Green paint added to the mix.

## PAINTING A RESIN BUILDING IN SEVEN STEPS

To show the different types of model building available today I have painted both MDF and resin

versions, in step-by-step guides. There are several important differences between them. The resin building shown in this project is produced by Hovels, who have been making fabulous buildings for the wargaming hobby for quite a few years now, and cover most periods of history. Hovels have an extensive American Civil War range, which is excellent in both variety and quality. These buildings are made from polyester resin with grey filler added; they are quite different to touch compared to the MDF kits, and require little or no assembly, depending on the model. The Hovels buildings also have more pronounced detail cast on them, which makes them nicely suited to washes and dry brushing.

The model in this step-by-step demonstration is a log cabin. As the MDF Dunker Church kit is whitewashed in real life, as were quite a few other American Civil War buildings, the brown of the wooden log cabin is an interesting alternative to demonstrate to you. (Other buildings produced by Hovels can be seen in many of the photographs in this book.)

### Step 1: Base shade for the cabin walls

*Colours:* Leather Brown, Saddle Brown, Flat Brown, Beige Brown and Bone White

This resin building did not need much cleaning up; use a scalpel and a small file to get rid of any small marks. You will need an old paintbrush to paint the base shade as the surface is quite rough and there are many indentations on the building as well. Mix together fairly equal amounts of Leather Brown, Flat Brown, Saddle Brown and Beige Brown on a painting

ABOVE: This model barn from Hovels is a great example of a quality resin building that can enhance your ACW wargames' terrain.

RIGHT: STEP 1: Painting the base shade of the walls.

STEP 2: Painting the highlight on the walls using Bone White and Ivory.

STEP 3: Painting the base for the roof and chimney.

tile, and paint the logs on the sides of the building with this mix. Make sure to paint the end of the roof as well in this colour. Once this is all done, give the brush a good clean and put it to one side.

Lastly paint the ends of the logs and round the windows using Bone White. This gives a good contrast with the darker brown and shows the wood inside the logs. When complete, give the brush a good clean and put it to one side.

## Step 2: Highlight for the cabin walls
*Colours:* Bone White and Ivory

Use Bone White as a highlight for the cabin walls. The building has a lovely texture cast on it, so it is ideally suited to dry brushing. It's important to keep brushes especially for dry brushing and for painting base shades, rather than spoiling smaller brushes that aren't suited to these tasks.

Pour the Bone White on to a mixing tile, and dip an old brush into the paint; then wipe off most of the excess paint on a cloth. Brush the remaining paint up and down the catch on the raised areas. You need to apply quite a bit of pressure when dry brushing to achieve a noticeable effect. Then dry brush the ends of the wooden logs using Ivory paint, taking care not to get too much on the darker areas that you have just painted.

## Step 3: Base shade for the roof and chimney
*Roof colours:* Beige Brown and Leather Brown
*Chimney colours:* Light Grey, Medium Grey and London Grey

Paint the roof tiles with a mix of Beige Brown and Leather Brown using a fairly large, old brush. Make sure paint reaches in between all the tiles, as it is important not to leave any grey showing. Also paint the edges of the tiles at the ends of the roof using this paint mix.

Paint the chimney with a mix of Light Grey, Medium Grey and London Grey. Although it's important to be as neat as you can most of the time, if there are little mistakes they can easily be painted over.

### Step 4: Highlights for the roof and chimney
*Roof colours:* Medium Grey, Ivory and Light Grey
*Chimney colour:* Ivory

Mix together Medium Grey, Light Grey and Ivory on the mixing tile to create a nice highlight colour. Dip the old dry-brushing brush in this mix, then wipe off most of the excess with a cloth. When dry brushing, brush the brush down the roof, and not across or up it. This is because the light falls downwards from the sun and the highlight colour will give the impression of light catching the edges of the tiles. It's important to wipe most of the paint off the brush before dry brushing, and to use quite a lot of pressure when dry brushing to give the right effect. The chimney was dry brushed with Ivory in exactly the same way as explained before.

### Step 5: Doors and windows
*Colours:* Black, Leather Brown, Beige Brown, Bone White and Silver

Paint the window frames and the door with a mix of Leather Brown, Beige Brown and Bone White, making sure there is no grey showing in between

STEP 4: Painting the roof highlights.

STEP 5: Painting the doors.

STEP 6: Applying
the washes.

STEP 7: Painting the final
details of the building.

the planks of the door. Once this has dried, paint the panes of the windows Black. Paint the front of the logs in the log pile using Bone White, then dab uneven patches of Beige Brown on top to create variety. Add the final details for this stage when you paint the horseshoe and lock for the door using Silver paint.

## Step 6: Applying washes
*Colours:* Dark Grey wash, Brown wash and Dark Green paint

By now the building is looking mostly done, but there is quite a lot of scope for different washes on a building of this type. Wash the walls with a mix of Dark Grey and Brown washes, applying it liberally over the whole of the side surface, including the windows and door.

Next give the chimney a Dark Grey wash, then paint uneven patches of Dark Grey and Brown washes on the roof. Do not mix these together, but apply them separately. Occasionally mix Dark Green paint with these washes to create areas of moss and algae that would be growing on the roof tiles.

Wash the woodpile in front of the cabin with a dark mix of Dark Grey and Brown washes.

## Step 7: Painting the base and final details
*Colours:* Blue, Flat Yellow, Bone White and London Grey

Much of the base will already be brown from where the washes and some of the earlier dry brushing have run down, so now just a few of the cast-on grass areas need attention. Paint these with a mix of Blue and Flat Yellow as an undercoat. Once this has dried, dry brush them with Flat Yellow, and then again with a mix of Bone White and Flat Yellow as a highlight. Dry brush the brown areas of the base with Bone White to help show the texture.

Next paint diagonal lines on the window panes with a fine brush using London Grey. This helps them stand out and gives the appearance of glass panes.

The final detail to add to this building is to dry brush the log pile with Bone White. This helps to separate the individual logs, making them look less like a solid object.

## CREATING THE WORLD IN MINIATURE

After the time and effort you have spent painting miniatures for your armies, it would be a real shame if they didn't have some quality terrain to fight over and to show them off to their best. This can be purchased or is fairly easy to make yourself. It's best to start off with the basics and build up the rest over time to include bridges, rivers and so on.

The most important part of creating the world that your troops will inhabit is detail. The real world is brimming with detail, and your tabletop will benefit enormously from some attention to detail on your terrain. You shouldn't have just one length of grass, but a variety of plants, trees and shrubs, all of different sizes and both alive and dead. Ideally it should represent a season, but for most wargamers this will be very limiting with the battles that can be fought. Most terrain is therefore aimed at spring and summer.

### Tips for Painting Fences

Painting this kind of scenery requires a less careful, almost careless approach to painting. A big brush to cover the areas quickly is best, taking care to cover all the small areas that are difficult to get at. Once the base colour has dried, then dry brush the fence with a pale highlight. Once this has dried, apply a dark wash all over. This will sink into all the recesses and bring out all the details on the model.

It is important to make sure the previous coats are well and truly dry before applying the wash, because if you don't, the colours will mix and become muddy and blurred. This will look most unattractive, so that extra bit of time ensuring the previous colour is properly dry is definitely worthwhile.

### Tips for Painting Walls

Painting walls is quite easy, but just like fences, you will need quite a few of them, so painting them as a batch of ten, for example, is a good idea. For undercoat, spray the walls grey using car primer, which saves a lot of time, and the paint is more likely to get into all the deeper recesses.

Once this has dried, brush a very pale grey highlight over the stones to catch all the raised edges. This doesn't have to be as neat as when you are painting a miniature: it doesn't matter if some stones are lighter than others, as this will give the walls a realistic natural look.

Once the highlights are dry, make a wash from a mix of Burnt Umber and Black, and wash it over all the stones. You will need to apply it liberally to ensure it reaches all the recesses. Once the wash has dried, paint the base earth colour, and dry brush and base it in the same way you would a figure.

The most important part of painting walls and fences and other similar pieces is the basing stage. As fences and walls are relatively dull items to look at, they need to be displayed on an attractive base to bring them to life. These models should be based with the same care as your miniatures, taking care to apply stones, tree branches, grass and flowers as you would apply details on your figures. With a little time and patience these small details are easily added, and really bring a bland model such as a fence or a wall to life. This attention to detail will make your wargames' table look fantastic!

## COMPANIES THAT PRODUCE GREAT SCENERY

The model trees and shrubs featured in the photographs throughout this book are available from www.themodeltreeshop.co.uk. Their miniature trees are excellent. The Model Tree Shop has a good selection of different species, which are available in different colours and sizes. This selection means that whatever scale of miniatures you choose to collect there will be something suitable for your table. The models are made of plastic, etched brass or twisted wire, while the leaves are made of various types of flock. The Model Tree Shop has an excellent mail order service as well.

There are now quite a few companies producing static grass and scenic tufts. These products are truly excellent quality, compared to the coloured sawdust that modellers were obliged to use in the past. We are very lucky with this improvement in the products available, as these items can really enhance your miniatures. Some of the static tufts and terrain elements used in this book are available from Tajima1 and War-World Scenics. Both companies produce great ranges of easy-to-use, quality products, and between them cover most of the styles you might need for your wargames' miniatures.

The Tajima1 grass tufts have tacky glue on them already, so all you have to do is peel them off and place them on the base. This company's ready-to-use scenic elements are superb – the scenic clusters contain a variety of different tufts, flowers and leafy shrubs, as well as static grass tufts in different lengths. They are quite big, but you can always trim them down to fit on bases. I do this on some of the bases of a regiment. Having the occasional base with

plenty of details on it really helps to complete the look of the unit.

War-World Scenics also produce a very attractive range of static grass tufts in a wide range of colours. Just like those produced by Tajima1, War-World

ABOVE: **A wonderful example of a hand-made tree, available from the Model Tree Shop.**

LEFT: **Tajima1 make fantastic ready-made scenic elements.**

Some examples of the grass tufts available from War-World Scenics

Scenics' grass tufts are made with tacky glue on the back of them, so they are very easy to use. Simply peel off the waxy paper they are supplied on, and use them on your miniatures. Most grass tufts can be dry brushed after they are applied to that base, which is a useful way to brighten them up or tone them down, depending on the effect you want.

Alternatively you could make your own grass tufts using the Flockbox from Warpainter, as shown in Chapter 7. When I discovered the Flockbox I was intrigued by the idea of trying to make my own modelling scenery. I have to say it is a brilliant gadget! It's fun and easy to use, and can also be used to apply static grass directly to a model or terrain board. The grass fibres will stand on end, giving a more realistic and professional look to the model you are working on. And by doing this yourself you can use static grass in colours and lengths of your choice, rather than be restricted by what is offered commercially.

# Conclusion

I COULD NOT HAVE written this book without the patience of my family, to whom I am indebted, as always. They are always there to support, counsel and encourage. In the course of writing this book I have discovered new products, and have sought where possible to show the reader a small selection of the wargaming products that are now available. My main aim has been to teach the novice painter the basic techniques used in creating wargames armies. It is not a book designed to teach showcase painting: if it was, there would probably

be better subject matter available for an individual miniature than the conservative uniforms of the American Civil War, such as a Polish winged hussar, Landsknecht or Aztec Jaguar knight, for example. The information contained in this book I hope will help you paint armies with which you can enjoy wargaming the American Civil War!

A lot of pleasure can be acquired from learning to paint figures and then expanding that knowledge over time. I have made miniatures professionally for twenty-two years and am always learning, even now.

Union regiments begin their advance.

A 28mm 146th NY Zouave charging, available from Steve Barber Models.
*PAINTED BY STEVE BARBER.*

I hope this book persuades the novice to get started in this fantastic hobby, and gives the seasoned painter some new ideas and the inspiration to expand their collection of figures. It has been a challenge for me to write, and has made me think once again about how I paint. Most of the time you never really analyse what you do when you're doing something, and probably take all the processes involved for granted. So perhaps it is a good thing to take a closer look every once in a while.

It has also given me the chance to showcase some of the fantastic products that are available for the American Civil War and for wargaming in general, some of which I was unaware of until I started writing this book.

The first challenge was what painting methods to use and how best to demonstrate them. There are many different ways to paint and all have their advantages and disadvantages. Over the years I have tried different styles and brands of paints and brushes, before settling on my chosen ones. I hope that the three main styles I have chosen to demonstrate give the novice wargamer in particular a good idea of the range of styles to choose from, and that those already familiar with painting figures will also see some useful ideas.

As a miniature painter, each figure you paint for your armies will give you experience, and this will help you when it comes to choosing colours, as well as perfecting details. The most important thing to remember is to enjoy painting your figures. It's never a good idea to force yourself to complete a painting project, as this will only serve to make you not want to paint. Painting can be calming when not forced. It is also a good way to de-stress and escape for a few hours. I suspect that is why most of us do it.

Once I started writing this book, the importance of scenery, scenic effects and terrain became increasingly apparent to me. With the help of some wonderful people I have been able to show you the fantastic scenic items, trees and grass tufts that were used in the photographs featured throughout this book. I have never analysed the products I use as much as during the process of writing this book, and I wanted to show you the best products I could find. Quality often lies in the details, and scenery is no exception. The scenery used on your wargames' table is, after all, the canvas your miniatures are displayed on, and good scenery will make your troops even more of a joy to look at and wargame with. This enjoyment will hopefully encourage you to paint more of them.

Wargaming is a hobby supported by great people, and most of us involved in it just want to encourage others to join in and enjoy this growing pastime. Many people who are not involved with the hobby don't realize how big it is now. If you are new to wargaming, then the American Civil War presents a perfect way to get involved without taking on anything too difficult to start with. On the whole the miniatures themselves are relatively easy to paint, and have plenty of character about them. That, and the easily accessible historical information, mean that for the beginner this is the perfect period to start with. It is one of my favourite periods of history, partly because of the misnomers. So much of the

knowledge that you have about the era before you begin, will end up being questioned the further you progress into the period.

The American Civil War was in reality a complex war fought for very individualistic reasons. It was also one of the last wars fought in the old Napoleonic style of regiments fighting in lines. By the end of the war a lot of the fighting was fought in trenches, making the American Civil War a precursor of World War I over fifty years later. The sacrifice of those who died during this conflict and in many other wars is often sadly forgotten. These men often died fighting for their brothers, and wargaming keeps the memory of these increasingly distant conflicts alive. Sometimes lessons can be learned from these seemingly distant conflicts, which can be applied today. After all, these were real people with real lives, so for me, wargaming is definitely not about glorifying war, but remembering it and learning from it.

Becoming a wargamer necessitates a certain amount of historical reading, mostly for uniform

A Union 12pdr battery in action.

details and battle formations. But most of the time you just pick things up as you plan and paint your new armies. Planning an army to paint involves working out what regiments were present at the battles you want to recreate, then finding the flags that your chosen regiments used, and so on. It certainly isn't essential to be a history buff to enjoy painting figures, but it's hard not to pick up information as you work on your troops and the colourful generals who led them. The important part of being a wargamer is that you just enjoy painting and gaming with miniatures.

Painting, like most things, is a mixture of technique, practice and personal taste, and you can often learn more from your mistakes than your successes. And once you start painting you will soon establish what contrasts and effects you like on your figures. And as we know, practice makes perfect: the more you paint, the faster and more accomplished at painting you will become.

When I first started painting miniatures, I read painting articles in magazines that inspired me to get into this hobby. I hope you have enjoyed reading this book, and that you will use some of the methods demonstrated in the step-by-step projects to paint your own figures. I must also say to all of the people who have helped me to complete this book, that I send you my heartfelt thanks. It has only reconfirmed to me what great people there are within the wargaming hobby. I hope readers of this book will find the photos of my collection of 28mm American Civil War miniatures inspiring and that this inspiration will help them to start painting and building their own collection of miniatures. And whether you are a painter, a wargamer, or a collector of miniatures, I hope you will get pleasure from this great hobby.

OPPOSITE PAGE:

TOP: A typical base of three 28mm Iron Brigade miniatures.

BOTTOM: The men of Virginia reach for their flag as the regiment's standard bearer falls, mortally wounded.

THIS PAGE:

The Confederate brigade commander orders his men to watch their flank as the Union troops charge!

Confederate infantry take the farm.

# Contact Details

WHILST WRITING THIS BOOK I became increasingly aware of the importance of showing readers some of the fantastic products that are available, to help them with the hobby of painting American Civil War miniatures. I realized they might like to know where to purchase figures, paints, scenery, tools and other items, and so I contacted a variety of companies, most of whom have contributed items that I have been able to show in this book. I am extremely grateful to all those who have helped in this way.

Vallejo
*Address:* A.P. 337 – 08800 Vilanova i la Geltrú Barcelona (Spain)
*Email:* info@acrylicosvallejo.com
*Website:* http://www.acrylicosvallejo.com

The Milliput Company Ltd
*Address:* Unit 8, Marion Industrial Estate, Dolgellau, LL40 1UU, UK
*Email:* info@milliput.demon.co.uk
*Website:* https://www.milliput.com

Sylmasta Ltd
*Address:* Halland House, Dales Yard, Lewes Road, Scaynes Hill, RH17 7PG, UK
*Email:* acvandamme@sylmasta.com
*Website:* https://sylmasta.com

Steve Barber Models Ltd
*Address:* 55 Golden Riddy, Linslade, Leighton Buzzard, Bedfordshire, LU7 2RH, UK
*Email:* enquiries@stevebarbermodels.com
*Website:* http://www.stevebarbermodels.com

War-World Scenics
*Address:* 30 Lonlas Village, Worksop, Skewen, Neath, SA10 6RP, UK
*Email:* info@wwscenics.com
*Website:* http://www.war-world.co.uk

Warpainter Scenics
*Address:* Furzebrook Studios, 52 Furzebrook Road, Wareham, BH20 5AX
*Email:* warpainter@btinternet.com
*Website:* https://www.warpainter.net

Sarissa Precision
*Address:* Thorpes Road, Heanor Gate Industrial Estate, Heanor, DE75 7EE, UK
*Email:* enquiries@sarissa-precision.co.uk
*Website:* https://www.sarissa-precision.com

Hovels Ltd
*Address:* 18 Glebe Road, Scartho, Grimsby, NE Lincs, DN33 2HL, UK
*Email:* sales@hovelsltd.co.uk
*Website:* http://www.hovelsltd.co.uk

Flags of War
*Address:* 42 Amulree Place, Glasgow, G32 7SW, UK
*Email:* info@flagsofwar.com
*Website:* http://www.flagsofwar.com

Battleflag
*Address:* 68 Goodison Blvd, Bessecarr, Doncaster, DN4 6DG, UK
*Email:* battle-flag@hotmail.com
*Website:* http://www.battle-flag.com

Loctite
*Address:* Henkel Ltd, Wood Lane End, Hemel Hempstead, Hertfordshire, HP2 4RQ, UK
*Email:* technical.services@henkel.co.uk
*Website:* www.loctite-consumer.co.uk

The Model Tree Shop
*Address:* The Model Tree Shop, 4 David Hume View, Heathgrange, Chirnside, Duns, TD11 3SX, UK
*Email:* steve@themodeltreeshop.co.uk
*Website:* https://www.themodeltreeshop.co.uk

Tajima1
*Address:* Tajima1 Miniatures, 72 Southgate Street, Redruth, Cornwall, TR15 2ND, UK
*Email:* tajima1minis@gmail.com
*Website:* http://www.tajima1.co.uk

East Riding Miniatures
*Address:* 1 The Woodlands, Goddard Avenue, Hull, HU52BW, UK
*Email:* ermtony@gmail.com
*Website:* http://shop.eastridingminiatures.co.uk

Shesto
*Address:* Sunley House, Olds Approach, Watford, Hertfordshire, WD18 9TB
*Email:* sales@shesto.co.uk
*Website:* https://www.shesto.co.uk

# Index

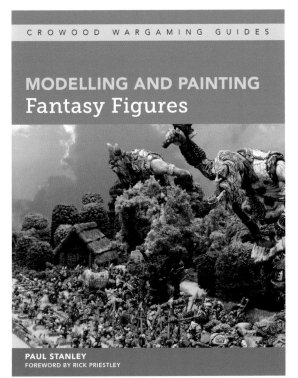

CROWOOD WARGAMING GUIDES

**MODELLING AND PAINTING**
Fantasy Figures

**PAUL STANLEY**
FOREWORD BY RICK PRIESTLEY

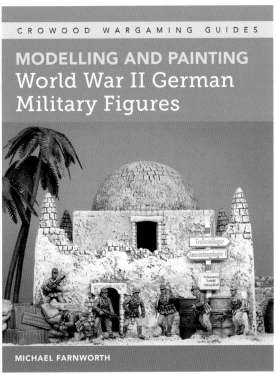

CROWOOD WARGAMING GUIDES

**MODELLING AND PAINTING**
World War II German
Military Figures

**MICHAEL FARNWORTH**